The Great Contradiction

The Great Contradiction

The Tragic Side of the American Founding

JOSEPH J. ELLIS

ALFRED A. KNOPF
New York
2025

A BORZOI BOOK
FIRST HARDCOVER EDITION
PUBLISHED BY ALFRED A. KNOPF 2025

Published by Alfred A. Knopf, a division of Penguin Random
House LLC, 1745 Broadway, New York, NY 10019.

Knopf, Borzoi Books, and the colophon are registered
trademarks of Penguin Random House LLC.

Library of Congress Cataloging-in-Publication Data
Names: Ellis, Joseph J., author
Title: The great contradiction :
the tragic side of the American founding / Joseph J. Ellis.
Other titles: Tragic side of the American founding
Description: First edition. | New York : Alfred A. Knopf, 2025. |
Includes bibliographical references and index.
Identifiers: LCCN 2024052407 |
ISBN 9780593801413 hardcover | ISBN 9780593801420 ebook
Subjects: LCSH: Slavery—United States—History | Indians, Treatment
of—United States | Indian Removal, 1813–1903 | United States—Race
relations—History | United States—Politics and government—1783–1865 |
United States—History—1783–1865
Classification: LCC E446 .E45 2025 | DDC 306.3/620973—dc23/eng/20250421
LC record available at https://lccn.loc.gov/2024052407

Maps by Jeffrey L. Ward

"PBS" is a registered trademark of the Public Broadcasting Service
and is used with permission. All rights reserved.

penguinrandomhouse.com | aaknopf.com

Printed in the United States of America
2nd Printing

The authorized representative in the EU for product safety and compliance
is Penguin Random House Ireland, Morrison Chambers, 32 Nassau Street,
Dublin D02 YH68, Ireland, https://eu-contact.penguin.ie.

To Stephen G. Smith,
in gratitude for over three decades of
editorial wisdom from the sharpest pencil
inside the Beltway

Contents

Foreword
The Way We Were

In the following pages we will be traveling back in time to a foreign country. It is a place called the American Founding, a popular destination for all American historians, including yours truly.

In fact, several of the following chapters draw heavily on previous visits to such historic cites as the Declaration of Independence, the Constitution, the ever-elusive mind of Thomas Jefferson, and that entire generation I chose to call *Founding Brothers*.

This trip, however, will be different. Our tour will focus on the downside of the American founding. While we will notice the triumphs in passing, our tour will focus on two unquestionably horrific tragedies the founders oversaw: the failure to end slavery, and the failure to avoid Indian removal.

We will assume from the start that we are witnessing a truly tragic moment. Less obvious is the kind of tragedy we are witnessing. Is it a Greek tragedy, meaning inevitable, unavoidable, "the will of the gods"? Or is it a Shakespearean tragedy, meaning avoidable, the product of inadequate leadership rooted in moral blindness?

As you will see, I have my own opinion on both tragedies. But the final verdict belongs to you. Whatever your verdict, generating a robust argument is the ultimate rationale for our trip. Argument itself is the prerequisite for a historically correct answer.

We could argue endlessly about which tragedy was more morally reprehensible, and all readers should feel free to do so in the privacy of their own minds. But there is no question that the debate over slavery had a much greater impact on the political and ideological values created at the American founding, including otherwise inexplicable compromises reached at the Constitutional Convention.

For that reason, the failure to end slavery commands more space in the pages that follow than the failure to avoid Indian removal. But there is another, more relevant reason to focus on slavery and its racist residue: namely, it connects the way we were then with the way we are now, as a society that continues to grapple with the political and even emotional implications of becoming a biracial or multiracial America. In effect, we are still living a story about the presumption of white supremacy that had its origins and first chapter in the American founding.

Part I

Overviews

—◦⦿◦—

Show me a hero and I will write you a tragedy.

—F. SCOTT FITZGERALD, *The Crack-Up* (1945)

To despise slaves as Negroes was redundant, but when Negroes were no longer slaves they became despicable as Negroes. The spate of manumissions after the Revolution tended to heighten the white man's distaste for Negroes as such. Certainly no one wanted them around.

—WINTHROP D. JORDAN, *White over Black: American Attitudes Toward the Negro, 1550–1812* (Chapel Hill, N.C., 1968)

Chapter 1

An American Dilemma

о о о

> Why increase the sons of *Africa,* by planting them in *America,* where we have so fair an opportunity, by excluding all blacks and tawneys, of increasing the lovely white and red? But perhaps I am partial to the complexion of my Country, for such kind of partiality is natural to Mankind.
>
> —BENJAMIN FRANKLIN,
> *Observations Concerning the Increase of Mankind* (1751)

IF HISTORIANS WERE ASKED to identify the greatest human tragedies of all time, the Holocaust would probably top the list, for reasons both powerful and plausible. In a short period of time, between six and seven million Jews were exterminated in Central and Eastern Europe. Unlike the higher mortality rates caused by plagues and pandemics, the Holocaust was a man-made event, a systematic program of unspeakable brutality conducted by otherwise civilized human beings.

A century before the Holocaust happened, the future prime minister of Great Britain Henry Palmerston provided his own answer to the same question: "If all the crimes which the human race has committed from the creation down to the present day were added together in one vast aggregate . . . ," he observed in 1844, "they would scarcely equal . . . the amount of guilt which has been incurred by mankind in connection with this diabolical slave trade."[1]

Palmerston was describing the Atlantic Slave Trade, also a systematic program of unspeakable brutality conducted by otherwise civilized human beings. But it was a much-longer-term tragedy, lasting for four centuries—roughly speaking, from 1460 to 1860. And it was, if you will, a sin committed by multiple nations, including Portugal, Spain, France, the Netherlands, Great Britain, and the United States. And for that very reason, it enjoyed long-standing and broad-gauged acceptance; nothing akin to the Nuremberg Trials occurred to judge and condemn the prominent slave traders. Great Britain did its penance by becoming the most ardent enforcer of laws against the slave trade on the high seas during the middle decades of the nineteenth century.

Almost four centuries earlier, Portugal had laid the foundation for the Atlantic Slave Trade, primarily because the superior design of Portuguese ships permitted captains to sail against the wind and down the western coast of Africa. Europe was "discovering" Africa at the same time it was "discovering" the Americas. Initially, the dominant presumption was that enslaved Native Americans would become a labor force for European nations. Instead, enslaved Africans became the labor force for European colonies in the Americas.

Portugal established the framework: coastal harbors from Senegal to Angola; inland routes, usually along rivers, reaching five hundred miles into the African interior; contracts with African tribal chiefs, who provided the human captives for a price that, on average, was less than half the price the enslaved Africans would fetch in Brazil. Everyone prospered: the Lisbon investors; the Portuguese government, which took a percentage of the profits; the merchant class; the African chiefs. The only losers were the enslaved Africans. Several papal bulls offered assurance that the suffering that Africans endured as slaves was more than justified by the eternal life in heaven they would enjoy as converts to Christianity.[2]

Over time, first the Spanish, then the French, then the British stepped into the African marketplace that the Portuguese had created. Although the word "capitalism" had not yet entered the lexicon, the Atlantic Slave Trade flourished for one elemental reason: it was the most lucrative investment available for Europe's merchants, bankers, and landed aristocracy. And until late in the game—the middle years of the eighteenth century—one would be hard-pressed to hear any criticism of such a flourishing enterprise. Moral blindness made eminent economic sense.

o o o

If demography is destiny, the Atlantic Slave Trade transformed the destiny of the entire Western Hemisphere. Between 1500 and 1800, five times as many Africans as Europeans were carried to the New World. Thanks largely to the recent work of British historians, who have created a digital database that provides the most accurate account ever assembled of the African diaspora, we now know much more precisely the scale and size of the Atlantic Slave Trade and where the enslaved Africans ended up.

Between 1550 and 1860, European vessels embarked with 12.5 million African captives and landed 10.7 million in the New World.* During the notorious Middle Passage, 1.8 million enslaved Africans died from some combination of disease, malnutrition, mistreatment, and suicide. Of the 10.7 million survivors, 4.8 million went to South America, 4.7 million went to the Caribbean,

---

* Another African diaspora in the other direction was occurring at the same time, even larger than the Atlantic Slave Trade. Between fourteen and sixteen million Africans were carried east, across the Sahara, over the Red Sea and Indian Ocean. Africa was plundered from the west by Christians and from the east by Muslims.

800,000 went to Central America, and 400,000 went to North America. (An additional 60,000 entered North America indirectly from the British West Indies.) In effect, only a small percentage of the enslaved Africans, about 4 percent, were deposited in the future United States.[3]

As a result, the Southern Hemisphere was destined to become a multiracial society including a population with African origins. The Northern Hemisphere was destined to become a predominantly white society with a substantial African minority. The term "African" is somewhat misleading, since the enslaved black population identified as Ashanti, Ebo, Igbo, Congolese, or other tribal affiliations, each with its own language, religion, and customs. In his monumental *African Founders,* David Hackett Fischer has documented in considerable detail the ways in which the different tribal origins of the enslaved population generated regional differences in the shape slavery assumed within the future United States.[4]

For obvious reasons, the vast majority of enslaved Africans were imported into the British colonies of North America only after Great Britain assumed domination of the Atlantic Slave Trade in the late seventeenth century. On the eve of the American Revolution, there were five hundred thousand slaves of African origin in the mainland British colonies—20 percent of the total population. Though the slave trade was still booming, a majority of the enslaved population were second- or third-generation residents, for whom Africa was a distant memory and English the dominant language. They had become African Americans, a term that entered the lexicon in 1782.[*] For that reason, when the plan to reverse the diaspora and resettle the emancipated slaves in Africa became a condition for emancipation, very few of the African Americans were willing to go voluntarily.[5]

---

[*] Since a majority of the white population in the United States arrived in the nineteenth and early twentieth centuries, African Americans as a group can trace their origins as Americans further back in time than a majority of Whites.

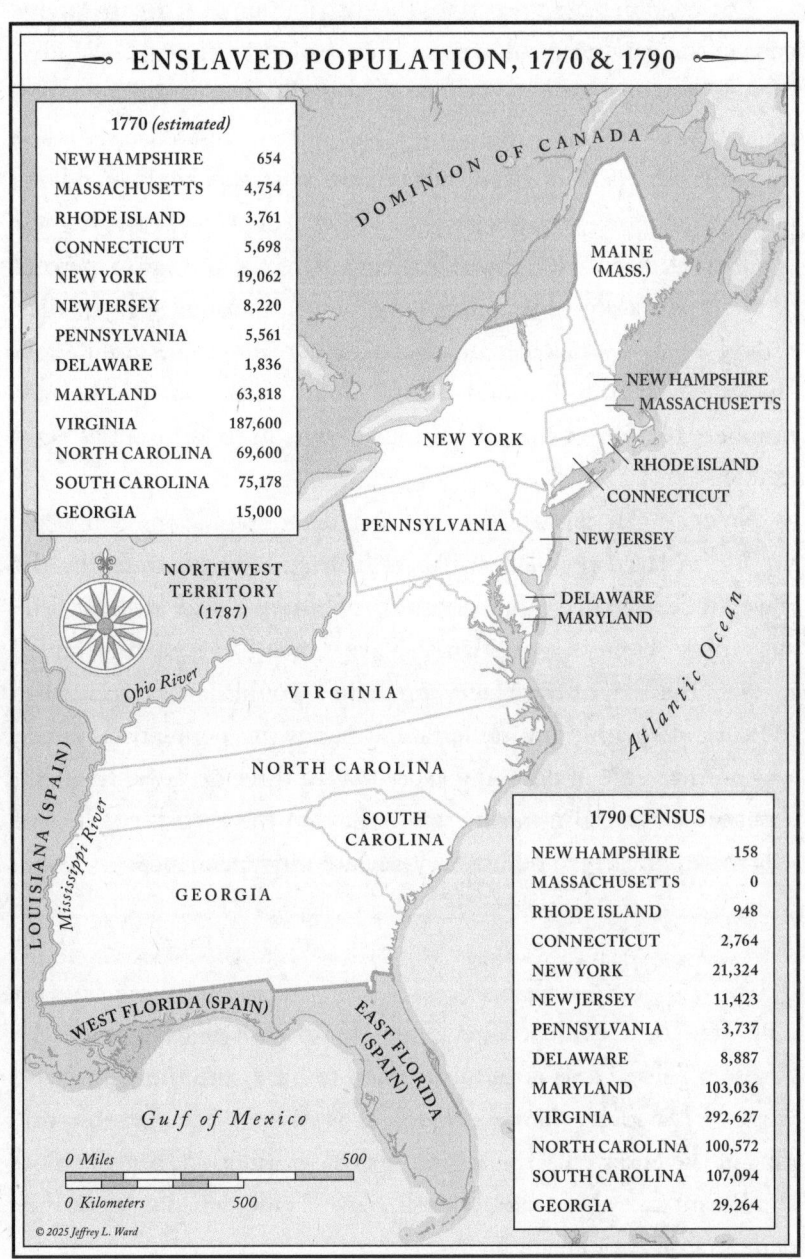

ENSLAVED POPULATION, 1770 & 1790

1770 *(estimated)*

NEW HAMPSHIRE	654
MASSACHUSETTS	4,754
RHODE ISLAND	3,761
CONNECTICUT	5,698
NEW YORK	19,062
NEW JERSEY	8,220
PENNSYLVANIA	5,561
DELAWARE	1,836
MARYLAND	63,818
VIRGINIA	187,600
NORTH CAROLINA	69,600
SOUTH CAROLINA	75,178
GEORGIA	15,000

DOMINION OF CANADA

MAINE (MASS.)

NEW HAMPSHIRE
MASSACHUSETTS

NEW YORK

RHODE ISLAND
CONNECTICUT

PENNSYLVANIA

NEW JERSEY

NORTHWEST
TERRITORY
(1787)

DELAWARE
MARYLAND

Atlantic Ocean

Ohio River

VIRGINIA

LOUISIANA (SPAIN)

Mississippi River

NORTH CAROLINA

SOUTH
CAROLINA

GEORGIA

1790 CENSUS

NEW HAMPSHIRE	158
MASSACHUSETTS	0
RHODE ISLAND	948
CONNECTICUT	2,764
NEW YORK	21,324
NEW JERSEY	11,423
PENNSYLVANIA	3,737
DELAWARE	8,887
MARYLAND	103,036
VIRGINIA	292,627
NORTH CAROLINA	100,572
SOUTH CAROLINA	107,094
GEORGIA	29,264

WEST FLORIDA (SPAIN)

EAST FLORIDA (SPAIN)

Gulf of Mexico

0 Miles	500
0 Kilometers	500

© 2025 Jeffrey L. Ward

African American population on the eve of independence

The map on page 7 describes the distribution of African Americans in the American colonies on the eve of independence. Approximately 10 percent of the black population lived in New England or the Middle Colonies, where most but not all were enslaved. The remaining 90 percent lived south of the Chesapeake, from Maryland to Georgia. Virginia was the largest colony with the highest number of enslaved African Americans, constituting 40 percent of the population. The number in South Carolina was smaller, though enslaved Blacks constituted 60 percent of the population. In Tidewater Virginia and coastal South Carolina, Blacks outnumbered Whites by a ratio of four to one, in some counties eight to one.

No map can capture the evolving demographic trend upward for the enslaved population. Apart from growth generated by the slave trade, the African American population had become self-sustaining. Even if the Atlantic Slave Trade had somehow ended in 1776, the size of the black population would have continued to increase at roughly the same rate as the white population, which was on the verge of doubling every two to three decades. In effect, a permanent racial minority was built into the British colonies of North America even before they declared independence.

ο ο ο

The statistical evidence generated by British historians of the Atlantic Slave Trade is certainly good to have, and the pioneering work of David Hackett Fischer on the diverse demographic origins of the enslaved Africans is a major contribution. But the most significant fact about the Atlantic Slave Trade defied statistical or demographic evidence.

We might call it the Great Silence. For more than four centuries, the most important voices of Western civilization remained mute as a highly organized program of unspeakable barbarity with genocidal implications flourished throughout Europe. Plato, Socrates, Aristotle, Aquinas, Erasmus, Locke, and all the Catholic popes regarded slavery and the slave trade as acceptable features of European society. Western civilization lacked a conscience.

Then, all of a sudden, in the middle decades of the eighteenth century, a chorus of voices condemning both the slave trade and slavery itself ended the Great Silence. In Europe the voices came from so-called *philosophes* in France, England, and Scotland, a movement led by intellectual elites, eventually called the Enlightenment, that demonized slavery as a vestige of the Dark Ages, when human reason was trapped in a cave of ignorance. Although the voices of Diderot, Voltaire, Montesquieu, Adam Smith, and David Hume were destined to play a significant role in the British colonies of North America during the American Revolution, prior to the war for independence the strongest voices opposing slavery and the slave trade came from religious leaders, chiefly Quakers and ministers of the "New Light" persuasion.[6]

For the secular *philosophes*, slavery was a medieval anachronism. For religious advocates of the "Inner Light" or "New Light," slavery was a sin. Human equality was rooted in the recognition that, as Jonathan Edwards put it, we are all "sinners in the hands of an angry God."

The most prominent revivalist preacher, George Whitefield, described white racism as a massive delusion. "Do you think you are any better by Nature than the poor Negroes? No, in no wise. Blacks are just as much, and no more, conceived and born in sin, as White Men are. Both, if born and bred up here, I am persuaded, are naturally capable of the same improvement." The leading Quaker orator, John Woolman, expanded on the same egalitarian message: "Placing on Men the Title, SLAVE, dressing them in filthy Garments, making them perform manual labour, in which they are often dirty, tends gradually to fix a Notion in the Mind that they are a Sort of People below us in Nature. This deprives the Mind as prevailing cold congeals Water."[7]

While the revivalist movement generated a potent emotional message among its followers—endorsing slavery or the slave trade was effectively purchasing a one-way ticket to hell—the Quakers created the framework for the first antislavery movement in the British colonies and, in fact, in the world. John Woolman led the way as an orator, but Anthony Benezet outdid him as a writer; his pamphlets most fully exposed the horrors of the Atlantic Slave Trade, so long suppressed, ignored, or erased from memory.

For example, Benezet described the screams as African families were split apart at slave auctions; the nonchalant way in which unhealthy slaves had their throats slit and were thrown to the sharks during the Middle Passage; the brutal execution of recalcitrant slaves in Jamaica, who had their legs and arms cut off before being burned alive. More than any other American writer, Benezet ended the Great Silence for an American audience. Over a decade before the onset of hostilities with Great Britain, Quaker meetings had initiated the practice of expelling all members who insisted on owning slaves or making a profit in the slave trade.[8]

ο ο ο

On the eve of the American Revolution, then, half a million African Americans, many in place for several generations, were permanently embedded in the North American population. The slave trade was flourishing, with record numbers of British slave traders docking along the southern coast. Charleston had become the emerging epicenter for imports; and the blooming rice and indigo economy in the South Carolina lowlands had become the chief market for slave labor. (Between 1760 and 1770, over fifty thousand Africans were landed in Charleston.) The following advertisement appeared in the Charleston newspaper on July 19, 1760: "To be sold, very cheap, on Tuesday at Strawberry Ferry, a choice cargo of about Two Hundred very healthy Negroes, of the same Country as are actually brought from the River Gambia." Instead of declining, the Atlantic Slave Trade to the future United States was growing exponentially.[9]

Meanwhile, although no such thing as a plan for emancipation was under consideration in any of the colonial legislatures, a robust antislavery movement was occurring "out of doors" at crowded religious revivals, in evangelical churches (chiefly of the Baptist and Methodist persuasion), and in Quaker meetings. The strength of this abolitionist movement, the first of its kind in world history, was its resolutely moral focus. The Great Silence was over. It was no longer possible to debate the slavery question with blissful indifference to the moral issues at stake. Looking ahead, a half-century later, William Lloyd Garrison would make the same nonnegotiable moral message the foundation of the second-wave abolitionist movement.

In the crucible of the moment, however, once the American Revolution put slavery on the political agenda, first-wave abolitionists had little to offer other than their moral certainty that slavery was a sin. For the underlying question became not whether slavery should be ended but how to do so without creating a biracial society.

There was a decidedly demographic dimension to that question, with a uniquely American question mark. For, once emancipation became a visible and viable prospect, American slaveowners were forced to face a racial reality that their counterparts in London, Paris, Madrid, and Lisbon could ignore. Namely, what would happen to the freed slaves? The enslaved population of all the European powers was located an ocean away in the Caribbean and Latin America. Not so the slaves in the former British colonies of North America, most of whom were long-standing residents on American soil. Quite quickly, the debate over slavery became an argument about the viability of a biracial society, an arrangement that enjoyed the support of only a tiny fraction of the white citizenry, and that no other nation in the world had ever embraced, much less achieved.[10]

In his *Notes of a Native Son* (1955), James Baldwin provided the most succinct assessment of the unique challenge that demography had forced upon American society: "The establishment of democracy on the American continent was scarcely as radical a break with the past as was the necessity, which Americans faced, of broadening the concept to include black men." The term "American exceptionalism" usually refers to some quasi-divine status of superiority enjoyed by the United States. More realistically, it accurately described the uniquely American challenge of coming into existence as a white-dominated biracial society that was rhetorically committed to human equality. This was the American dilemma long before Gunner Myrdal gave it a name. And, to a surprising extent, it still is.[11]

Chapter 2

Angles of Vision

o o o

We hold these truths to be self-evident, that all men are
created equal. . . .

—THOMAS JEFFERSON,
The Declaration of Independence (1776)

I have never seen, to my knowledge, a man, woman, or child,
that was in favor of producing a perfect equality, socially
and politically, between the negro and white people.

—ABRAHAM LINCOLN,
The Lincoln-Douglas Debates (1858)

THE FOUNDING ERA IS the Big Bang in the American
political universe. In one compressed moment during the
last quarter of the eighteenth century, the American colonies won their independence from Great Britain, announced to
the world the enlightened values on which their bold experiment
in republican government rested, created the first nation-sized
republic in modern history, and established the political institutions designed to preserve and protect republican principles for the
foreseeable future. These achievements made the United States the
political model of the liberal state, which displaced the monarchical dynasties of Europe in the nineteenth century, then rescued

Western civilization from the totalitarian despotisms of Germany, Japan, and the Soviet Union in the twentieth.

Most of these achievements were unprecedented, and perhaps the largest achievement of all was to shift the tectonic plates of Western political thought by insisting that power did not flow downward from God to monarchs and then feudal aristocracies, but instead flowed upward from that quasi-mystical entity called "the people" to their elected representatives. Small wonder that the British philosopher Alfred North Whitehead observed that there were only two occasions in Western history when the political elite of an emerging empire behaved as well as anyone could reasonably expect: the first occasion was Rome under Caesar Augustus; the second was the United States under the founding generation.

All of the above can justifiably claim to be the historical truth, but it is not the whole truth. For there are two legacies of the founding era that must be noticed, and both qualify as enormous tragedies. Alongside their impressive achievements, the founding generation failed to reach a just accommodation with the Native American population, and failed to end slavery or, more realistically, put it on the road to extinction. Both failures led directly to horrific consequences: a policy of genocide in slow motion for Native Americans; and the bloodiest war in American history to end slavery.

Taken together, these triumphal and tragic elements constitute the ingredients for an epic historical narrative that defies all moralistic categories, a story rooted in the coexistence of grandeur and failure, brilliance and blindness, grace and sin. No aspiring historian could wish for more. It cries out for a protégé of Henry Adams to expose the ironies of it all: the overlapping ways that achievements on one side of the political equation closed off options on the other side; how leaders trapped in contradictions invented denial mechanisms to avoid facing their hypocrisy; how some of the wisest men of our greatest generation became mentally paralyzed once race entered the conversation. In this narrative format, all saints are also sinners (Thomas Jefferson is a singular figure who leads the list in both categories), the high moral ground turns out to be a utopia—Greek for "nowhere"—and all the gods are laughing.

But that is not the way the story has been told. Instead, we have been asked to choose between two competing narratives of the founding. One features the founders as demigods who were permitted to glimpse the eternal truths, or, as Ralph Waldo Emerson once put it, "to see God face to face." The other is crowded with a cast of despicable villains who collectively comprise the deadest, whitest males in American history. These mindlessly celebratory and naïvely judgmental responses to the founders are in fact complementary cartoons, the front and back sides of the same childlike portrait that we periodically rotate, like adolescents fluctuating between the emotional imperatives of unconditional love and Oedipal hate.

◦ ◦ ◦

My own efforts during the past four decades have been dedicated to rescuing the founders from the electromagnetic field we have constructed around them. It seemed self-evident to me from the start that the mythology surrounding the revolutionary generation was a fog bank that needed to be blown away. Charles Francis Adams, the grandson of John Adams, made the point most succinctly long ago: "We are beginning to forget that the patriots of former days were men like ourselves. And we are almost irresistibly led to ascribe to them in our imaginations certain gigantic proportions and superhuman qualities without reflecting that this at once robs their character of consistency and their virtues of all merit."[1]

What seemed self-evident to me seemed misguided and almost sacrilegious to a surprising number of self-described history buffs, who regarded the words "God shed his grace on thee" as sacred script. It dawned on me gradually that, for the same reason that religions require divinely inspired prophets, emerging nations seem to require mythological heroes. Think Ulysses for Greece, Romulus and Remus for Rome, King Arthur for England. Such legendary figures, all fictional characters, link the messy uncertainties of nation building to a transcendent region of certainty and truth that defies criticism and doubt. It is what William James called "the will to believe."

For that reason, it made patriotic sense to capitalize the Founding Fathers, construct temples to them on the Mall and Tidal Basin, carve their faces into Mount Rushmore. During the formative phase of the infant American republic, when its survival was still problematic, iconic founders performed a valuable function as reliable sources of unquestioned wisdom, a veritable gallery of Delphic oracles available on demand.

The mythologized version of the founding encountered early opposition from prominent members of the revolutionary generation, who registered their disbelief that the all-consuming crisis they remembered so well was being transformed into a childish fairy tale. John Adams led the way, brandishing his customary irreverence: "It is a common observation in Europe that nothing is so false as modern history," Adams observed. "And I should add that nothing is so false as modern history except modern American history." In the Adams formulation, the true history was about chance, contingency, and unintended consequences, about political leaders who were all improvising on the edge of catastrophe. Perhaps he had missed it, he joked, but no member of the Continental Congress represented a colony called Mount Olympus. In an effort to display his own modesty—not a natural act for Adams—he made a point of objecting to his own sanctification: "Don't call me 'Godlike Adams,' 'The Father of His Country,' or 'The Founder of the American Empire.' These titles belong to no man, but the American people in general."[2]

∘ ∘ ∘

Ah, "the American people in general." There it is, the great rallying point in American history, the secular equivalent of heaven, the place to go when all else fails in the search for an impregnable political fortress that no patriotic American would dare to attack.

As far as the American founding is concerned, it is a lie—or, if you prefer less disturbing language, a massive delusion. None of the prominent founders believed they were creating a democracy. In fact, the term itself was an epithet throughout the founding era, a way to describe ignorant and easily deceived popular majorities, perpetually vulnerable to demagogues. The last quarter of the eighteenth century was a pre-democratic era, and all efforts to read a Jacksonian or Tocquevillian faith in the wisdom of the common man into the American founding are misleading distortions.

The political lodestar for the revolutionary generation was not "the people" but, rather, "the public," as in "res publica," or public things. In that world, the public interest seldom coincided with popular opinion. The public interest was the long-term interest of the people, which a majority of people at any given time seldom comprehended, mostly because they were born, lived their lives, and died within a three-hour horse ride. They could not think nationally or, as Hamilton preferred, continentally, because their mental horizons were quite literally limited by their day-to-day experience of life. During the war for independence, they strongly supported local militia units, but refused to extend that support to the Continental Army.

The point merits mention as we prepare to engage the tragic side of the American founding, since the dominant assumption within the American political universe is that democracy is always an asset for the side committed to worthy causes. The exact opposite was true when it came to avoiding Indian removal or ending slavery. Any political movement to achieve those goals needed to come from the top down rather than the bottom up. Why? Because a sizable portion of the white population sought to pursue their happiness by acquiring land occupied by Native Americans. And an even larger proportion of the same segment of American society, even those willing to contemplate the abolition of slavery, could not imagine a post-emancipation America of racial equality as anything but a nightmare.

o   o   o

If the original sin of American history is slavery, and racism its toxic residue, the original sin for American historians is "presentism," the presumption that our political and moral values now are wholly reliable standards of truth and justice for the assessment of our predecessors then. Think of the Christian missionary who wonders why her prospective African converts have never heard of Jesus.

The British historian Herbert Butterfield coined the term "the presentistic fallacy." "The study of the past with one eye, so to speak on the present," he wrote, "is the source of all sins and sophistries in history, starting with the simplest of them, the anachronism. It is the fallacy into which we fall when we are giving the judgments that seem the most assuredly self-evident." For our purposes, a historical rather than presentistic approach must regard the founding era as a foreign country, and all inhabitants of that place in time can only be assessed, much less judged, after we have internalized their values and prevailing assumptions. Any trip back in time that begins as a quest for heroes or villains is fatally flawed from the start. Much like structural racism, presentism is an embedded presumption of moral supremacy to be avoided at all costs.[3]

Avoiding this fallacy is not an easy thing to do. The founders have become valuable trophies in the ongoing culture wars, ardently claimed by both sides. The pro-American side emphasizes the triumphs, airbrushes out the tragedies, and veers close to patriotic mythology. The anti-American side focuses exclusively on the tragedies, usually makes slavery the chief argument for the prosecution, and dismisses the triumphs as hypocritical rhetoric. Both sides think more like lawyers than historians, deriving their satisfaction from scoring points as advocates for their respective clients. Nothing is lost in this interpretive framework except historical truth in its most disarming configurations.

○ ○ ○

And so, as we prepare to travel back in time to that foreign country called the founding, there are three false trails that need to be marked at the start, three misguided assumptions virtually certain to lead us astray.

First, the prominent founders were neither demigods nor devils, and embracing either stereotype tells us more about ourselves than it does about them. Second, our understandable affection for democracy must be put aside, in part because the founding generation did not share our faith in "the people," and in part because the vast majority of white people then—even more so than now—embraced racial presumptions and prejudices that rendered the prospects of an emancipated black population unimaginable. Third, the moralistic agenda that some historians brandish so proudly is both fatally flawed and richly ironic, the former because might-have-been history is not really history at all, the latter because the egalitarian assumptions they celebrate all had their origins in the founding era they seek to demonize.

The late, great historian of slavery, David Brion Davis, even coined a phrase, "the perishability of revolutionary time," designed to remind us of the almost boundless optimism generated by the war for independence. "As later antislavery writers looked back upon the Revolution," Davis observed, "they discovered a time of selfless commitment, when the people possessed the willpower to assume that all problems, no matter how huge, were solvable. It was therefore imperative to act while individual and national feelings were still alive to the principles of justice and human equality."[4]

Such ideological exuberance was obviously unsustainable, which was Davis's main point. Any effort to put slavery on the road to extinction had to happen while the revolutionary embers were still glowing, before memories of what they called "The Cause" faded into the middle distance.* Whether they knew it or not, the window of opportunity to implement the egalitarian agenda of the American Revolution was closing.

Virtually all the prominent founders were thinking in the opposite direction. From their perspective, any frontal assault on slavery put at risk the political unity necessary to win the war, then to assure southern support for a nation-sized republic. Slavery was the self-evident contradiction that must be lived with until the infant American republic survived infancy. From their perspective, deferring the slavery issue rendered the triumphs of the founding possible; confronting it frontally rendered them impossible. Those enamored with the idea that justice delayed is justice denied might consider the alternative scenario provided by the French and Russian revolutions, where justice imposed led to justice destroyed, in France taking the form of the guillotine and Napoleon, in Russia the firing squad wall and Lenin, then Stalin. If the founders had done what some of my colleagues have denounced them for not doing, the American republic we currently and proudly inhabit would never have come into existence.[5]

The only way to end slavery at the founding was to create a federal government empowered to make domestic and foreign policy

---

* The term "The Common Cause" originated as a rallying cry for all the colonies to unite in support of Massachusetts in 1774. By 1776, "The Cause" came to mean unity behind the commitment to independence. During the war, the meaning expanded to mean the egalitarian values the troops were fighting for.

for the states. The only way to assure that a Constitution possessing such powers was ratified was to keep slavery off the agenda. The only way to understand the thought process of the most prominent founders is to inhabit that dilemma.

o   o   o

If we move to a higher altitude, we will be witnessing the first chapter in a long-standing American story. Let's call it the back-lash pattern. Briefly put, every step forward toward racial equality generates a backlash from a significant portion of the white population. What Martin Luther King called "the arc of the moral universe" is really an undulating up-down syndrome. It is an inherently paradoxical pattern, since racism surges only after some semblance of racial equality becomes foreseeable.

We should recognize the pattern when it first appears during the American founding, because we are currently living through its most recent manifestation in the movement to "Make America Great Again." And we should expect to see it again in or about 2045, when demographers predict that the white population of the United States will become a statistical minority.

Part II

Contexts

———◦∞◦———

We hold these truths to be self evident, that all men are created equal, that they are endowed by their Creator with certain inalienable Rights, that among these are Life, Liberty, and the pursuit of Happiness.

—THOMAS JEFFERSON,
The Declaration of Independence (1776)

Chapter 3

The Contradiction

○ ○ ○

If these solemn truths, uttered at such an awful crisis, are *self-evident*, unless we can show that the African race are not men, we can hardly express the amazement which naturally rises on reflecting that the very people who make these pompous declarations are slave owners.

—DAVID COOPER, *A Serious Address . . . on . . . Slavery* (1778)

I N 1763, GREAT BRITAIN became the British Empire. What was called the Seven Years' War in Europe and the French and Indian War in America ended with the Treaty of Paris, which transferred all French possessions in North America from the Mississippi to the Atlantic and Canada to Florida into British hands. The victory was so lopsided that ordinary inhabitants of England seemed baffled at inheriting a strange new world. "What have we done?" asked one anonymous writer who styled himself "Cato." As far as he could tell, "we now have from the Gulf of Florida to the North Pole, and how far West I really do not know." Most of his English friends, he explained, could not tell the Mississippi from the Danube, or the Alleghenies from the Alps. Were these acquisitions new jewels in the British crown, or new burdens to bear in the shape of taxes and military obligations?[1]

A more managerial perspective came from Francis Bernard, then serving as the royal governor of Massachusetts, who sensed a dramatic shift in the global templates. As Bernard saw it, Britain's policy toward the American colonies for the preceding century was not to have a policy, what Edmund Burke subsequently called "salutary neglect." In his *Principles of Law and Polity, Applied to the Government of the British Colonies in America* (1764), Bernard argued that the era of complacent negligence obviously needed to end. "This is therefore the proper and critical time," Bernard urged, "to reform the American governments upon a general constitutional, firm, and durable plan." The American colonies had been floating like thirteen distant planets in their own orbits, and now needed to be moved within the gravitational field of London and Whitehall. And if the British government failed to consolidate its control over its American cousins, Bernard warned, it was virtually inevitable that they would drift into their own independent orbits.[2]

The measures the British ministry took over the next decade to implement Bernard's imperial vision generated a reaction that eventually produced the very outcome that Great Britain sought to avoid. From the British perspective, their goal was perfectly sensible, to make the thirteen American colonies into reliable partners within the expanded British Empire. That meant making the inhabitants into second-class British citizens—in effect, into colonists.

From the American perspective, the British political initiative had more sinister implications. The entire white population was at risk of being relegated to a status previously associated only with enslaved Africans. Unintentionally, inadvertently, the moral perspective on slavery previously confined to Quaker meetings and evangelical churches moved to the center of the political arena.[3]

Within that arena, a veritable chorus of voices emerged in response to Parliament's inspired initiative, all singing the same song, doing so in remarkable harmony. A gallery of American writers, most of them lawyers, all of them previously obscure, seemed to pop up out of nowhere, up and down the Atlantic coast, between 1764 and 1774. The major players were: James Otis and John Adams in Massachusetts, Stephen Hopkins in Rhode Island, Daniel Dulany in Maryland, Richard Bland and Thomas Jefferson in Virginia, and John Dickinson in Pennsylvania.[4]

The core of the American argument has been summarized succinctly in four words: "No taxation without representation." While technically accurate, the summary is misleading, since it implies that the major American concern was economic. But just as the British rationale for imperial reform was not primarily financial, the American critique of British policy was not about taxes per se. In both cases, the deeper issue was about power and control, neither of which could be resolved by accountants juggling the numbers.[5]

From the British perspective, if their American colonies were permitted to drift along without guidance from London and Whitehall, their ultimate destination would be independence. And if the American colonies did depart the British Empire, it would set off a chain reaction, an early version of the "domino theory," since Canada, the Caribbean, and even India were likely to imitate the American example. From the American perspective, if they accepted the unprecedented doctrine of Parliament's sovereignty, they effectively surrendered control over their own lives. In retrospect, each side was exaggerating the threat posed by the other; each side was framing its arguments in nonnegotiable terms that, taken together, amplified the fears of the other side, generating the political version of a death spiral.[6]

o o o

James Otis of Massachusetts launched the American side of the argument in his pamphlet *The Rights of the British Colonies Asserted and Proved* (1764). Otis argued that American rights derived from two sources: first, those rights guaranteed in the British constitution for all British citizens; second, those rights from which the British constitution itself derived—namely, natural rights, a much more expansive region for which his primary source was Montesquieu's *The Spirit of the Laws* (1748).

By crossing the line from British rights to natural or human rights, Otis was effectively lifting the lid on Pandora's box, making all persons, regardless of race, class, or gender, recipients of the same rights. Quoting Montesquieu, Otis posed an explosive question: "Is it right to enslave a man because he is black? Will short, curl'd hair like wool help the argument? Can any logical inference in favor of slavery be drawn from a flat nose, a long or short face?"

Otis defined slavery as "being under the power and control of another as to our actions and properties." It happened that the same definition applied to the new British version of "colonist." Which led Otis to the inescapable conclusion that all the high-sounding British rhetoric about essential reforms was nothing less than "a plot to enslave us." The phrase soon became a refrain throughout the resistance movement up and down the Atlantic coast.[7]

By framing the argument against British policy in such stark terms—freedom against slavery—the leading voices of the American resistance transformed a political conflict over their rights as British citizens into a battle to the death to avoid enslavement. A still-obscure Virginia planter named George Washington was quick to catch the potency of the expanded American argument. "The crisis has arrived when we must assert our rights, or submit to every imposition that can be heaped upon us," he explained to a friend, "until customs and use make us as tame and abject slaves as the blacks we rule over with such arbitrary sway." Washington seemed to be saying that his experience as a slaveowner at Mount Vernon enhanced his understanding of the fate awaiting him if and when those he called "our Lordly Masters of England" had their way. He did not notice, or preferred not to mention, that he was vulnerable to the same argument that he was hurling at the British.[8]

That awkward fact did not escape the attention of England's most acerbic wit and literary lion. Samuel Johnson's defense of British policy, entitled *Taxation No Tyranny* (1775) was designed as a polemic against American upstarts, who were described as "ungrateful wretches" and "a race of rattlesnakes." But near the end of his diatribe, Johnson delivered his most famous line: "Why is it that we hear the loudest yelps for liberty from the drivers of negroes?"[9]

Patrick Henry had the misfortune to receive a personal letter from Anthony Benezet posing the same question. The most eloquent Quaker advocate of emancipation urged Henry to recognize that, as one of Virginia's most stalwart patriots, he was accusing Great Britain of the very atrocity he was committing as a slave-owner. He was, whether he knew it or not, living a lie.

Henry's response was a bewildering mixture of denial and guilt. "Would anyone believe that I was a Master of Slaves of my own Purchase?" he asked rhetorically. "I am drawn along by the General inconvenience of living without them," he admitted, "but I will not, I cannot justify it. I will so far pay my devoir to Virtue, as to own the excellence & rectitude of her Precepts & to lament my want of conformity to them." In short, he was not living a lie so much as a contradiction, and though he did not like to acknowledge that fact, once he had done so, he would continue to live the contradiction rather than live without his slaves.[10]

Both the logic and the language of the American resistance to British rule rendered entrenched apathy impossible to sustain. The American argument placed a huge question mark beside any government or institution that claimed the arbitrary power to control its constituents without their consent. And it rendered silence in the face of such presumptive power a treasonous act. From a more panoramic historical perspective, ideas and values about human equality entered the American political atmosphere for the first time, and have been reverberating there ever since.

"Blush you pretended votaries for freedom," wrote one New England minister, "ye trifling patriots who are making a vain parade of being advocates for the liberties of mankind while trampling on the sacred natural rights and privileges of Africans; for while you are fasting, praying, nonimporting, resonating, resolving, and pleading for a restoration of your charter rights, you at the same time are continuing this lawless, cruel, inhuman, and abominable practice of enslaving your fellow creatures."[11]

After Parliament passed the Coercive Acts (1774), when the British army occupied Boston and imposed martial law on Massachusetts, a Congregationalist minister in Rhode Island, Samuel Hopkins, claimed that God was sending all American colonists a clear warning: "Was not Boston the first port in the Continent that began the slave trade, and are not they the first shut down by an oppressive act, and brought almost to desolation?"[12]

The same point was made by an anonymous writer in the Philadelphia newspapers one year later: "How just, how suitable to our crime is the punishment which providence now threatens us? We have enslaved multitudes, and are now threatened with the same fate." The anonymous author, it turned out, was Thomas Paine, only recently arrived from England, soon to publish *Common Sense* (1776), again anonymously, but eventually recognized as the most compelling voice of the American resistance movement.[13]

o o o

Both the language and the logic of the American argument against British imperial policy enjoyed a receptive audience in Quaker meetings, and in many New England congregations, for its inescapable antislavery implications. Such was not the case, however, in more secular venues like the Virginia House of Burgesses.

In 1769, a first-year delegate named Thomas Jefferson drafted legislation that allowed the owners of slaves to free them without requiring permission from the governor or the legislature, as Virginia law then required. Because of his junior status, Jefferson deferred to a senior colleague, Richard Bland, to present his bill to the full House. He then watched as Bland was buried beneath an avalanche of invective for raising the prospects of emancipation in a public forum. According to Jefferson, Bland's career never recovered, nor did Jefferson ever forget that he himself would have suffered the same fate had he presented his own bill. Anyone even suggesting that emancipation was on the political agenda in Virginia was committing political suicide. In the Old Dominion, it turned out, freedom was colored white, and slavery was colored black.[14]

Letters to the editor of *The Virginia Gazette* (Williamsburg) during the ensuing weeks revealed a deep and widespread level of racial prejudice in the white population at large that had previously lain dormant, primarily because declarations of black inferiority had been unnecessary as long as the African population was safely enslaved. But the mere suggestion that emancipation was under consideration lifted the lid on the latent racial and racist convictions lying beneath the surface of Virginia society, even among white planters who owned few if any slaves.[15]

Here is one example, among many, of the popular backlash against any plan for permitting black slaves into Virginia society as equal members: "It is well known that our African slaves are not fully human. God formed them in common with Horses, oxen, dogs, and for the benefit of the White people alone to be used by them for their Pleasure, or to Labour with the other Beasts." The writer went on to claim that anyone familiar with the history of Africa knew that it was "a story of relentless barbarism, tribal wars, and moral darkness."[16]

One prominent American historian, Edmund Morgan, has ar-

gued that the presence of an enslaved black population actually
enhanced the commitment to freedom by the white population of
Virginia. It was not just that living with slavery made prominent
Virginians like George Washington and Thomas Jefferson more
aware of what British domination would resemble. Morgan also
suggested that less prominent Virginians were spared the task of
performing manual labor, since enslaved blacks filled that role,
thereby allowing all white Virginians to unite racially instead of
being divided into upper and lower classes, as was the case in
England and throughout Europe.[17]

Virginia was the largest colony—recall that it included present-
day Kentucky and West Virginia—and also boasted the largest
economy and a planter class that enjoyed disproportionate influence throughout the founding era. As a result, Virginia was destined to become the crucial state in the American debate over the
role of slavery in the early republic. For that very reason, it needs to
be noticed from the start that the overwhelming majority of white
Virginians presumed that their own freedom depended upon an
enslaved black population of inherently inferior human beings.
And that the tenure of any political leader who dared to challenge
that presumption would be of short duration.[18]

What we might call the "great contradiction" continued to
hover over the American argument against British imperial policy
throughout the late 1760s and early 1770s. Although New England
ministers and Quaker leaders often made the contradiction the
centerpiece of their sermons, with a few exceptions the colonial
legislatures were conspicuously silent on the awkward issue. That
silence ended in the fall of 1774, when fifty-six delegates from
twelve colonies met at Carpenters' Hall in Philadelphia as the First
Continental Congress.

From the very start of their deliberations, the delegates knew
they had a mandate to provide a united front in support of Massachusetts, where the British had imposed martial law after Parlia-

ment's passage of the Coercive Acts. The British effort to isolate Massachusetts as the designated epicenter of the American rebellion effectively backfired, generating a heretofore nonexistent demonstration of intercolonial unity. Independence was not yet on the American agenda; in fact, the delegates were searching for a way to avoid that outcome by imposing a boycott on all British imports, hoping that economic pressure might bring Parliament and the British ministry to their senses.[19]

The delegates quickly agreed that the boycott would include "any Goods, Wares, or Merchandise from Great Britain or Ireland"—in effect, everything. Then a separate paragraph announced the inclusion of all imported African slaves on the boycott list. It declared, "We will not import or purchase any slave imported after the first day of September next, after which time we will wholly discontinue the slave trade." In one nonchalant sentence the delegates seemed to resolve a problem that would bedevil subsequent delegates in Philadelphia thirteen years later, at the Constitutional Convention. What had just happened?[20]

The short answer is that we do not know. Neither the documentary records nor the correspondence of the delegates provides any account of their deliberations on the slave trade. Indeed, the silence is probably the strongest evidence that the issue was too controversial for the delegates to permit exposure, given the paramount priority of unity to what had come to be called The Common Cause or, more simply, The Cause.

We know that South Carolina was on record as opposing any restriction on slave imports. We also know that rice was the one commodity left off the boycott list of exports, and that South Carolina was the chief exporter of rice. So it is plausible to regard the rice exception as a political reward to South Carolina for joining the consensus on the slave trade.

We are only guessing, but another unspoken negotiation between Virginia and South Carolina seems both plausible and likely. We know that Virginia was already on record for ending the slave trade, not for moral reasons, but because Virginia's plantations were overstocked. So the planter class there stood to benefit if and when a domestic slave trade replaced the Atlantic trade as the chief labor source for burgeoning low-country plantations in South Carolina.[21]

What had the appearance of a significant step forward on the slavery issue was, at best, a sideward step motivated by the desire to inflict maximum pain on the British economy, and dominated at every stage by realistic political calculations by all the affected players. Moral considerations had no role to play in the deliberations.

Indeed, although slavery was a clear contradiction of The Cause, it was also a clear threat to the fragile coalition of colonies gathered together in Philadelphia as the self-appointed voice of the American resistance to British rule. It was simultaneously the unmentionable ghost at the banquet, for any explicit mention of slavery threatened to destroy the united front necessary for The Cause to succeed.

Moreover, as a preview of coming attractions, the political compromises brokered to end the slave trade exposed the inherently unrevolutionary character of what came to be called the revolutionary generation. Unlike Robespierre in France, Lenin in Russia, or Mao in China, the leaders of the American resistance were not utopian visionaries but, rather, an assemblage of pragmatic statesmen accustomed to negotiating the space between ideals and realities in their respective colonial governments. At least on the face of it, to speak of "prudent revolutionaries" is disconcerting, for it does not fit into the historical pattern established by all the prominent revolutionary movements in the modern world.

o o o

John Adams became the purest embodiment of a "prudent revolutionary" by insisting, earlier than most of his colleagues in the Continental Congress, that The Cause meant nothing less than American independence, but also nothing more than that—which is to say nothing about ending slavery, and nothing about whatever inspirational meanings the term was generating "out of doors," beyond the enclosed confines of the congress. "I am grieved to hear of this Rage for Innovation," he lamented to a Boston friend, and added, "These ridiculous Projects are not repairing, but pulling down the Building when it is on Fire, instead of laboring to extinguish the Flames. These radical Projects being bandied about in County Assemblies and town meetings tend directly to Barbarism."[22]

What "radical Projects" was he talking about? One was a proposal to end the property qualification to vote forwarded to him by Elbridge Gerry, an old Massachusetts friend. "Laws and Government are founded on the Consent of the People," read the proposal, "and that consent should be held by each member of Society as a right," otherwise "he is an absolute excommunicate." Adams denounced the proposal as a recipe for anarchy. "There will be no end to it," Adams warned. "New claims will rise. Even women will demand a Vote."[23]

Shortly thereafter, almost as if she were listening, Adams received a letter from his ever-"saucy" wife, Abigail. "And by the way," she began,

> in the new Code of Laws which I suppose it will be necessary for you to make, I desire you would Remember the Ladies, and be more generous and favourable to them than your ancestors. Do not put such unlimited power into the hands of Husbands— Remember all Men would be tyrants if they could. If particular care and attention is not paid to the Ladies, we are determined

to foment a Rebellion, and will not hold ourselves bound by any Laws in which we have no voice or Representation.[24]

John initially thought that Abigail was being playful, not really serious, and he responded with his own playful effort at mockery, claiming that everyone knew that women were the true tyrants within the household, and that he had no intention to exchange what he called "the tyranny of George III for the despotism of the petticoat." Bantering in this fashion was a fixed feature of their correspondence, but in this instance, Abigail wanted him to know that she could banter and still be deadly serious. There was nothing playful in her next letter:

> I can not say that I think you very generous to the Ladies, for while you are proclaiming Peace and good will to all Men, Emancipating all Nations, you insist upon retaining an abso-lute Power over Wives. But you must remember that Arbitrary power is like most things that are very hard, very liable to be broken, and not withstanding all your wise Laws and Max-ims, we have it in our power not only to free ourselves, but also to subdue our Masters and without Violence, throw both your Natural and legal authority at our feet.[25]

Abigail was envisioning not just the day when women would enjoy the right to vote but the end of patriarchy itself. At least in her mind, The Cause carried within its train the seeds of an American Revolution for all women.

The third and final "radical Project" that came flying at Adams lacked the personal potency of his beloved partner's feminist vision—this long before the word itself entered the political lexicon—but arrived as a veritable chorus of voices insisting that slavery was an obvious violation of the values embedded in The Cause.

An anonymous writer from Virginia minced no words: "Is it not incompatible with the glorious struggle America is making for her own Liberty, to hold in absolute Slavery a Number of Wretches in defiance of all we claim for ourselves?"

Another correspondent, signing as "Unknown," suggested, "Once the war is won, emancipation should be our first goal." Once the slaves were freed, the owners should be compensated by the profits acquired in selling land in Canada, which would almost certainly be annexed to the union during the war.[26]

In the same vein, but with a more compelling voice, came the following question from "Humanity": "What has the negros the africons done to us that we should take them from their own land and mak them sarve us to the da of thar deth? God forbid that it should be so anay longer."[27]

These plaintive condemnations of slavery reflected the antislavery dialogue within Quaker meetings and New Light congregations that had been going on for several decades. But they also exposed a more secular surge across a much broader political front. The surge was generated by the core convictions of The Cause, which stigmatized any and all institutions based on coercion rather than consent. Once that way of thinking was released into the political atmosphere, the meaning of The Cause kept expanding past long-standing barriers, to include patriarchy, the property qualification to vote, and, most offensive of all, slavery. Indeed, by the winter and spring of 1776, the entire reform agenda for the next century of American history had risen to the surface.

If The Cause was becoming an American Revolution, Adams assumed that his chief task was to make it happen in slow motion or to make, if he could have named the political movement he wished to lead, an "American Evolution." As he put it to the writer and activist Mercy Otis Warren, "I have ever thought it the most difficult and dangerous Part of the Business to contrive some method for the colonies to glide inevitably from under the old Government into a peaceable and contented submission to a new one." In the Adams political universe, justice delayed was not denied but, rather, deferred until it could "glide insensibly" into place. By the same token, justice imposed was a recipe for utter chaos, a society in which the very concept of justice lost any meaning.[28]

o   o   o

In this context, and in keeping with its own conservative instincts, the Continental Congress voted to appoint a thirteen-man committee, one delegate from each colony, to design the framework for a post-independence American government. In effect, before taking the great leap of independence, responsible revolutionaries should know where they were going to land. The committee was named after its designated chairman, John Dickinson, probably the most reluctant revolutionary in the congress.

The Dickinson Draft has confounded historians for centuries, because it bundled together a series of compromises between delegates with fundamentally different visions of post-revolutionary America. Until now, these differences had been suppressed in order to maintain a united front against British policy. But once independence was assumed, and thereby removed from the political equation, the chorus became a cacophony.

There were four fundamental disagreements: first, an argument between proponents for a confederation of sovereign states and advocates for a more consolidated national union; second, a division between large and small states over representation, whether it should be state-based or based on population; third, a split between states with claims to western land and those "landless" states lacking such expectations; and fourth, a sectional clash between northern and southern states over slavery. In effect, all the political and constitutional questions that would bedevil the emerging American republic for most of the next century were thrown onto the agenda for the first time.[29]

There was a clear consensus that slavery was a taboo topic with the explosive potential to blow up any pretense of political unity, thereby making a mockery of any "band of brothers" gathered under a patriotic canopy called The Cause. But it quickly became clear that slavery was too embedded in the economy of the southern states to be avoided altogether.

The forbidden topic came up in the debate over Article 12 in the Dickinson Draft, which proposed that "the expenses for the war and the general welfare shall be defrayed out of a Common Treasury, which shall be supplied by the several colonies in proportion to the Number of Inhabitants of every Age, Sex, and Quality, except Indians." An argument then ensued about how to count "Inhabitants," which quickly became an argument over slaves. Were they persons or property?[30]

The southern delegates insisted that slaves were property, like horses and sheep, and should not be counted as "Inhabitants" for the purpose of assessing the tax burdens in the southern states.* When that argument came before the full congress, Benjamin Franklin ridiculed the southern claim, observing that, the last time he looked, slaves did not behave like sheep: "Sheep," he joked, "will never make any insurrections." This bit of humor was not appreciated by the South Carolina delegation, which proceeded to issue the ultimate threat: if slaves were defined as persons, "there is the End of the Confederation."[31]

Eventually, both northern and southern delegates recognized the need to deflect the slavery question altogether by revising the

---

* At the Constitutional Convention eleven years later, the southern states reversed their position, arguing that slaves be counted as persons, because making slaves "Inhabitants" increased the size of their delegation in the House of Representatives. What became the three-fifths compromise in 1787 represented a recovery of the political solution previously proposed during the debate over the Dickinson Draft and then the Articles of Confederation.

Dickinson Draft to make tax assessments based on the value of land within each state rather than on population. This proved an attractive compromise, since land assessments were easy to manipulate downward, thereby reducing the tax burden on all the states. Most important, the compromise took slavery off the table. That was obviously the highest priority, for failure to do so risked losing the southern states, and without the southern states, victory in any war for independence became problematic.[32]

Less obviously, but with major implications for the slavery dilemma, the debate over the Dickinson Draft exposed a widespread political consensus that the common commitment to The Cause was regarded as a temporary arrangement. Because loyalties remained local and at most state-based, it was assumed that, once the war was won, all political power would flow back to the states, where it properly belonged. Indeed, any vision of a fully empowered national government conjured up a domestic version of Parliament, the same kind of faraway leviathan they were rebelling against.[33]

o o o

History was happening at an accelerating pace throughout the summer of 1776. On June 7, Richard Henry Lee of Virginia moved the resolution "that these United Colonies are, and of right ought to be, independent States." (Note the state-based assumption underlying the rationale for independence.) Congress decided to delay a vote on Lee's resolution until July 1 in deference to delegations requiring guidance from their respective state legislatures. In the meantime, a five-member committee was appointed to draft a document announcing American independence to the world if and when Lee's resolution won approval. No one knew it at the time— more pressing events were occurring in the still-undecided Pennsylvania and New York legislatures, not to mention the landing on

Staten Island of the first wave of the British invasion force under General William Howe—but the congress had just appointed the most consequential committee in American history.

On June 11, John Adams, Thomas Jefferson, Roger Sherman, and Robert Livingston met with Benjamin Franklin in his quarters. After Franklin declined the assignment, explaining that he had vowed never to write a document that would be edited by a committee, the group chose Jefferson to prepare a draft, which he proceeded to write in his Market Street apartment during the second week of June. He then shared his draft with Adams and Franklin; later, he recalled, "They were the two members [of] whose judgments and amendments I wished most to have the benefit." They suggested one minor revision, replacing "sacred and undeniable truths" with "self-evident truths." The committee delivered the document to the Continental Congress on June 28. This is actually the scene depicted in the iconic painting by John Trumbull; which most viewers think is the signing ceremony on July 4, which in fact never occurred.[34]

After voting unanimously on July 2 in favor of Lee's resolution (New York abstained), the delegates put themselves into committee-of-the-whole format to debate Jefferson's draft of the Declaration. No record of the debate exists, because none was kept. They made more than eighty editorial changes, revising or deleting over 20 percent of the text. Almost all the changes occurred in the long list of grievances against George III, in which Jefferson prosecuted the British king for violating the colonists' rights as Englishmen, thereby severing the only remaining connection with the British government. Nothing in this prolonged indictment bore directly on the slavery issue, except for one lengthy paragraph, which his fellow delegates deleted altogether, presumably because it raised the unmentionable subject, perhaps because it was the most incoherent piece of prose that Jefferson ever wrote.

He has waged cruel war against human nature itself, violating its most sacred rights of life and liberty in the persons of a distant people who never offended him, captivating and carrying them into slavery in another hemisphere, or to incur miserable death in their transportation hither. This practical warfare, the opprobrious of INVIDEL powers, is the warfare of the CHRISTIAN King of Great Britain. Determined to keep open a market where MEN should be bought and sold, he has prostituted his negative for suppressing every legislative attempt to restrain this execrable commerce. And that this assemblage of horrors might want no fact of distinguished die, he is now exciting those very people to rise in arms against us and to purchase that liberty of which he has deprived them by rendering the people on whom he has obtruded them, thus paying off former crimes against the liberties of one people, with crimes which he urges them to commit against the LIVES of another.[35]

One way of reading the deleted paragraph is to view it as a message aimed primarily at a Virginia audience. The Virginia legislature was on record for ending the slave trade, since their plantations were overstocked, and they stood to benefit if the Carolinas and Georgia became customers in a domestic version of the slave trade. So Jefferson's condemnation of the Atlantic Slave Trade as a moral travesty was politically popular in the Old Dominion. The claim that George III was "exciting those very people to rise in arms among us" referred to a proclamation by the royal governor of Virginia, Lord Dunmore, that offered freedom to all Virginia slaves who rallied to the British cause. By denouncing Dunmore's offer of emancipation, Jefferson seemed to contradict his own critique of George III for allegedly imposing slavery on the American colonies. None of this made rational sense.*

---

* See the next chapter for a more expansive treatment of the Dunmore episode.

It did, however, make a kind of revolutionary sense to fold slavery into the list of grievances against George III, using the political crisis to create a patriotic storyline in which an evil king imposes a diabolical institution on innocent and unwilling colonists. This, of course, was a preposterous piece of patriotic propaganda, but in the superheated moment, when blaming George III for a long train of abuses had become rhetorically possible and politically mandatory, adding slavery to the bill of indictments was an inspirational act. After all, since the occasion called for an indictment of the British king, why not add slavery to the list of criminal offenses, thereby laying the political foundation for emancipation in the document declaring America's own emancipation from British tyranny?

That question became a purely rhetorical concern as soon as the delegates in the congress deleted the entire paragraph. There were surely stylistic reasons for the decision: the convoluted syntax, strange word choice, operatic tone, all of which were out of place in a diplomatic document. Even Jefferson, the proven master of the written word, apparently lost his customary control when trying to mention the unmentionable. But, at least in retrospect, his instincts were excellent: the impulse to declare to the world that slavery was inherently incompatible with America's founding principles, and to blame the whole problem on a discredited British king.

o o o

Because most delegates were fixated on the lengthy indictment of George III and the argument that he had violated their rights as Englishmen, they ignored altogether the second paragraph of the Declaration, presumably regarding it as a mere rhetorical overture. For understandable reasons, they focused their attention on the pressing matter of the moment, which was whether to take the final step, the long-deferred leap toward independence, in the process risking, as Jefferson rather eloquently put it, "our lives, our fortunes, and our sacred honor." They were looking straight ahead, not gazing upward at the political stratosphere. As a result, they ignored altogether what were destined to become the fifty-six most important words in American history:

> We hold these truths to be self-evident, that all men are cre-ated equal, that they are endowed by their creator with certain unalienable rights, that among these are Life, Liberty, and the pursuit of Happiness. That to secure these rights, Governments are instituted among Men, deriving their just powers from the consent of the governed.[36]

Jefferson's mind did its best work at high altitudes, where his verbal fluidity also found its comfort zone. These talents allowed him to smuggle, in plain sight, the core principles of the natural-rights philosophy into the seminal document of the American founding. No less a figure than Abraham Lincoln, who could rival Jefferson in his way with words, put it most poignantly: "All honor to Jefferson, to the man who, in the concrete pressure of a struggle for national independence by a single people, had the coolness, forecast, and capacity to introduce into a merely revo-lutionary document, an abstract truth, applicable to all men and all times, and so to embalm it there, that today, and in all coming days, it shall be a rebuke and a stumbling block to the very harbin-gers of re-appearing tyranny and oppression." One can only assume that Lincoln was smiling when he wrote "a merely revolutionary document."[37]

Lincoln also called attention to another covert feature of Jef-ferson's magic words—namely, that they floated in a timeless zone far above the pressing demands of the moment. "The assertion that 'all men are created equal,'" Lincoln wrote, "was of no practical use in effecting our separation from Great Britain, and it was placed in the Declaration, not for that, but for future use." More specifically, although Jefferson's words were self-evidently incompatible with slavery, that obvious fact remained unspoken. A basic human right was being declared, but enforcement of that right was being deferred. Eternal principles could not be scheduled.[38]

Jefferson also inserted covertly antislavery language into the futuristic paragraph when he revised the trinity of rights most famously proposed by John Locke in his *Second Treatise on Government* (1690). Instead of "life, liberty, and property," Jefferson wrote "Life, Liberty, and the pursuit of Happiness." He borrowed the new phrase from George Mason, who had used it in his draft of the Virginia Constitution as a supplement to Locke's "property." By dropping "property" altogether, Jefferson deftly deprived slave-owners of the claim that owning slaves was a natural right protected by law. On this score, there can be little doubt that Jefferson knew what he was doing.[39]

For the rest of his life, Jefferson complained about the revisions made in his draft of the Declaration. ("Mangled" was his customary complaint.) But the manglers had left the natural-rights paragraph untouched. Over the years, as the meaning of Jefferson's words expanded, advocates of the abolition of slavery, women's rights, then racial equality and gay rights came to regard them as the semi-sacred core of the American promise, the only words in the Declaration of Independence that really mattered.

Chapter 4

Unpainted Pictures

o o o

I know not what course others may take, but as for me, give
me liberty or give me death!

—PATRICK HENRY, speech at the Virginia Convention,
March 23, 1775

There is not a man of them but would leave us, if they
believed they could make the escape.

—LUND WASHINGTON to George Washington,
December 3, 1775

W AR IS AN INHERENTLY ugly human creation that
blatantly defies our most cherished convictions about
humanity itself. For that very reason, the real war seldom makes it into the history books, and most wars come down
to succeeding generations in fictionalized versions: glorified and
mythologized by the winning side; falsified and forgotten by the
losers. The war for American independence fits that description
on both counts. No war in American history is more romanticized.
And no war in British history is more ignored.[1]

The chief source of our distorted version of the war—indeed, of
the entire founding era—is visual, in the paintings of John Trumbull, Charles Willson Peale, John Singleton Copley, and Gilbert

Stuart. Because the eighteenth century predated the camera, there are no Mathew Brady photographs of battlefield carnage, as in the Civil War; no films like *Saving Private Ryan* that realistically depict the chaos of combat in World War II.[2]

Although Trumbull did considerable research for all his battlefield paintings, he was self-consciously fitting the war into an epic framework that, as Abigail Adams put it, "will transmit to Posterity characters and actions which will command the admirations of future ages, give birth to them and prevent them from ever passing away into the dark abyss of time." American art historians have echoed Abigail's analysis ever since. The real war could never get into the books, because the pictures had already shaped the story to exalt and obscure.[3]

In Trumbull's battlefield masterpiece, *The Death of General Warren at the Battlefield of Bunker's Hill* (1785), Joseph Warren is depicted as an updated version of Hector of Troy, the heroic martyr posing for posterity. Warren was a prominent Boston physician—in fact, the doctor of Abigail and John's family—who had risen in the ranks of the Sons of Liberty to become a major figure in the American resistance. In the battle, he had held his ground during the first two British assaults. When the third wave overran his trench, he was shot in the back of the head while retreating down the hill, and was probably dead before he hit the ground. Trumbull falsified the death scene, making it the centerpiece of the painting, thereby assuring Warren's immortality as the first martyr to The Cause a full year before America declared its independence.[4]

Trumbull had his inspirational agenda, so there was no way he could possibly foresee our interest more than two centuries later in the racial makeup of the American army at the misnamed Battle of Bunker Hill. But, in one quite inadvertent way, he did. Far off to the right side of the picture, a partially obscured African American carries a musket. His name was Asaba, and he was serving alongside his wounded master, Thomas Grosvenor. He is the sole representative of the roughly 150 black soldiers who fought at Bunker Hill—some, like Asaba, manservants accompanying their masters; others as free Blacks in local militia units. In the first and one of the bloodiest battles of the war for American independence, the American army was racially integrated.[5]

Three weeks after Bunker Hill, when the recently appointed George Washington assumed command of the soon-to-be called Continental Army, he was surprised to see Blacks serving alongside Whites. After consulting with his senior officers, Washington issued an order "to reject all slaves and to reject Negroes altogether." The Continental Congress endorsed the decision, adding, "Neither Negroes, boys unable to bear arms, nor old men unfit to endure the campaign are to be enlisted."

Within a few weeks, however, when new recruits failed to fill the ranks as militia units disbanded, Washington was forced to change his mind. "It has been represented to me," he observed, "that the free Negroes who have served in the army are very much dissatisfied at being discarded." Moreover, there was reason to believe that, once released, they might go over to the British army. "I have therefore decided to depart from the Resolution respecting them," Washington reluctantly acknowledged, "and have given license for them being enlisted; if this is disapproved of by Congress, I shall put a stop to it."[6]

In this halfhearted, backhanded fashion, the same man who owned about two hundred slaves at Mount Vernon established the precedent for a racially integrated Continental Army. If only in retrospect, it was the first step in a long personal journey for Washington. The precedent also proved to be the first step in a long American journey—indeed, the only occasion when Blacks and Whites served alongside one another in integrated combat units until the Korean War.

In his pioneering work on the topic, Benjamin Quarles estimated that about five thousand African Americans bore arms in the Continental Army or the state militias during the war for independence. Subsequent scholarship has tended to confirm or slightly increase Quarles's estimate, though all agree that the scattered and incomplete character of the sources makes accuracy impossible. The trend, however, is quite clear. The longer the war went on, the more reluctant the state governments became to fill their designated quota of troops, and the more African American volunteers filled the gap, especially among those enlistees who agreed to serve "for the duration." By the end of the war, slightly more than 10 percent of the Continental Army were African Americans. There were 150 black troops at Bunker Hill, nearly a thousand at Yorktown. To the extent that the Continental Army served as the face of battle for The Cause, it was possible to believe that The Cause itself was becoming biracial.[7]

o   o   o

If we shift our focus to the states south of the Potomac, where 90 percent of the African American population resided, a quite different picture begins to form. It is a picture in which ten to twelve thousand Blacks served in the British army during the course of the war, twice as many as served in the Continental Army, though not in combat units. The picture first began to congeal in Virginia five months after Bunker Hill, when Lord Dunmore, the recently exiled governor of Virginia, issued a proclamation offering freedom and the protection of the British navy to all runaway slaves who joined his small flotilla off the Virginia coast. Within three weeks, more than eight hundred escaped slaves had arrived and volunteered to serve in what Dunmore called his Ethiopian Regiment. Although his untrained volunteers got mauled by Virginia militia outside Norfolk, the flow of runaways kept coming, to include the wives and children of the early arrivals. What was happening?[8]

The short answer is that the pent-up urge for freedom that

had been building for decades in the slave quarters at last had a place to go. Prior to the outbreak of the war, escaped slaves in Virginia lacked a safe destination. There were no thick jungles where they could hide forever like the Maroons in Jamaica. The Underground Railroad lay almost a century away. Escaped slaves were almost always recaptured, punished with public whippings, and, if they proved recalcitrant, condemned to serve in Virginia's iron mines, effectively a death sentence. Dunmore's proclamation not only provided a previously unavailable safe harbor for runaways, it also flipped the central American argument for independence on its head. Suddenly, Great Britain was simultaneously threatening white Virginians with slavery and providing enslaved Virginians with a path toward freedom.

The sheer size of the exodus to Dunmore's offshore haven had ominous implications for Virginia's planter class: namely, that they were sitting atop an active volcano on the verge of eruption. If the British government, following Dunmore's example, chose to recruit and mobilize the enslaved population by offering them freedom, the consequences could be catastrophic, especially in the Tidewater counties, where Blacks outnumbered Whites three to one.

One young Virginia statesman, who still styled himself James Madison, Jr., put it most succinctly: "We shall fall like Achilles by the hand of one who knows the secret." Dunmore had exposed the secret, which was that the huge enslaved population in the Old Dominion was the Achilles' heel of The Cause. (Madison preferred classical references to volcanic metaphors.) In fact, all the colonies south of the Potomac were vulnerable to slave insurrections, driven by the same argument for human freedom that was being hurled at the British government as the rationale for American independence.[9]

Only a month before Dunmore's proclamation, the former governor of South Carolina William Lyttelton rose in the House of

Commons to recommend a southern strategy for the looming war, based on the very vulnerability that Madison found so ominous. Trading on his previous experience in the region, Lyttelton argued that a British invasion of the southern colonies would generate massive insurrections by the enslaved population. If several royal regiments invaded Virginia or the Carolinas, "the negroes would rise and wash their hands in the blood of their masters." The current preference of the British ministry for a northern strategy, initially aimed at New York, needed to be reconsidered. The southern colonies were the soft underbelly of the American resistance.[10]

Lyttelton's argument was greeted with a barrage of invective during the debates in the House of Commons. The mere suggestion that the British government would encourage slave insurrections in the colonies was "too horrid and wicked to be heard of, much less adopted by a civilized people." Even the idea of arming slaves and allowing Blacks to serve alongside Whites in the British army was ridiculed as "a policy almost designed to generate indignation and horror among veteran troops." Everything Lyttelton proposed, and that Dunmore subsequently attempted to implement, defied the moral principles the British Empire claimed to stand for.[11]

The hypocrisy seeping out of the cracks in this upright posture defied measurement. Great Britain at the time was the leading slave trader in the world, and many representatives in the Commons were wealthy slaveowners with vast holdings in Jamaica and Barbados, who had more in common with Virginia's planter class than with any putative cluster of moral principles. The stated aversion to recruiting African Americans is also intriguing, since the British ministry was currently negotiating with several tribes in the Iroquois Confederacy to bolster the size and strength of the British army. And George III was deciding to spend a small fortune to enlist mercenaries from several Germanic principalities to serve alongside British regulars. One can only conclude that, beneath the moralistic veneer, the British government was extremely reluctant to align itself with any policy that had explicit antislavery implications, or that treated Blacks as equal to Whites.*

As far as the runaway slaves in Virginia were concerned, the debates in Parliament could be happening on the moon, and the thought that they were the front edge of a slave insurrection never occurred to them. From their perspective, they were escaping enslavement, poised to pursue whatever opportunity presented itself, and quick to conclude that Dunmore's little fleet was the closest thing to the promised land that the fates had ever provided. Complicated political considerations were not part of their calculations. If the Virginia legislature had offered them freedom in return for enlistment in the state militia, they would have seized that opportunity with equivalent enthusiasm. But the Virginia legislature never gave that option any consideration.

By the early summer of 1776, as the vote on American independence approached, the exodus of slaves declaring their own independence was continuing apace. Dunmore's flotilla expanded to over a hundred ships in order to accommodate the steady stream of new arrivals, which now included as many women and children as men. Up in New England, John Adams expressed his amazement at the speed and reach of the communication network within the enslaved communities. "The Negroes have a wonderful art of communicating intelligence among themselves," he wrote in his diary, estimating that "it will run several hundred miles in a week or a fortnight."[12]

---

* In 1772, Chief Justice Lord Mansfield granted freedom to James Somerset, a Jamaican slave who had escaped into London's small free-black community. Mansfield ruled that English law was incompatible with slavery in the British Isles, though the ruling had no impact on slavery in the Caribbean or North America, where the vast majority of British-owned slaves resided. It would take another half-century for Great Britain to end slavery throughout the British Empire. Several otherwise competent American historians have misread Somerset to mean that Great Britain was committed to abolishing slavery during the war.

But stories in the Virginia press soon began to report hundreds of black bodies floating ashore, initially suggesting, with apparent glee, that Dunmore had decided to feed the sharks. In fact, the front edge of a widespread smallpox epidemic was hitting Virginia, and African Americans were more vulnerable to the disease than Britons, who had developed some semblance of immunity after several decades of exposure to the virus, which had never struck Africa. The consequences were catastrophic for Dunmore's refugees, who began dying at a faster rate than new arrivals could replace them. In order to isolate the infected runaways, Dunmore eventually decided to move his base to Gwynn's Island, off the Virginia coast, but the disease outran his efforts to control it. Within a matter of weeks, over half of his roughly one thousand escaped slaves were dead and the other half dying. Dunmore was forced to leave them behind and sail north toward the Chesapeake with the small remnant of healthy survivors.[13]

When Virginia militia and accompanying reporters arrived on Gwynn's Island, they witnessed a scene out of Dante's depiction of hell. Dead bodies were lying one atop another over an area two miles long. The pungent stench from the decaying corpses was still in the air, and the dying were crawling over the dead while crying for water. For obvious reasons, no American artist at the time saw fit to depict the scene, and no American director ever since has chosen to feature it in a film about the American Revolution. If one is looking for martyrs, however, the dead and dying African Americans were martyrs to their own compelling version of The Cause, which gave a new kind of meaning to Patrick Henry's famous phrase: "Give me liberty or give me death!"[14]

In the moment, however, the threat posed by Dunmore reverberated throughout the planter class in Virginia—not the scene of escaped slaves dying horrible deaths on some obscure island, but the picture of an Ethiopian Regiment, numerous and armed, marching toward isolated plantations with revenge in their hearts.

Any Virginia planter who harbored doubts about the wisdom of war with Great Britain quickly discovered a powerful reason to abandon those doubts.

One prominent Virginia delegate to the Continental Congress, Richard Henry Lee, put it succinctly: "If the British Administration had searched through the whole world for a person best fitted to ruin their cause, they could not have found a more complete agent than Lord Dunmore." The historian Woody Holton has even made the case, exaggerating only slightly, that "no document, not even Thomas Paine's *Common Sense* or the Declaration of Independence, did more than Dunmore's proclamation to convert the white residents of Britain's more populous American colony to the cause of independence."[15]

Like an airburst in the night, the Dunmore threat exposed a southern version of The Cause. We might think of it as The Cause with a southern accent. Its defining distinction was the unspoken but broadly shared assumption that the egalitarian values of The Cause applied only to Whites. The surprising size and scale of Dunmore's movement terrified the planter class, because it demonstrated how contagious the urge for both freedom and equality was among Blacks, who were not supposed to think that way—indeed, like horses and sheep, they were not supposed to think at all. One nonevent was also extremely revealing. In response to Dunmore's proclamation, no prominent Virginian proposed that the House of Burgesses counter Dunmore's offer with an offer of freedom for enslaved Blacks who volunteered to serve in the Virginia militia. Within the Virginian political universe, the most self-evident truth of all was white supremacy.[16]

o o o

It was quite a scene. Of all the paintings that we would like to have, all the visual opportunities that cry out for a camera, the movement of the Continental Army into its winter quarters at Valley Forge on December 19, 1777, ranks at or near the top of the list.

One eyewitness, Private Joseph Plumb Martin, entitled the scene "A Cavalcade of Wild Beasts." He described twelve thousand barefoot soldiers trailing a ribbon of blood on the snow as far as the eye could see. The line of march included 750 African Americans, all free Blacks from northern states. One of them, a former slave named Jethro, was barely able to walk, and was found facedown in his tent on Christmas Day, the victim of exposure and malnutrition. Roughly twenty-five hundred black and white soldiers would join Jethro in the hereafter over the next six months, along with five hundred horses, whose decaying carcasses generated a smell that filled the air when they unfroze in the spring. Bringing up the rear of the march were about five hundred wives, mothers, cooks, washerwomen, and prostitutes. Taken together, the entire assemblage of struggling souls made Valley Forge the third-largest city in North America, after Boston and Philadelphia.[17]

Washington confirmed the desperate condition of his soldiers in a letter to Henry Laurens, the new president of the Continental Congress. The miserable status of the army defied description, he claimed, and "must be seen to be believed." What's more, the misery "was beyond my power to relieve or prevent." He concluded with an ominous warning: "I am now convinced beyond a doubt, that unless some great capital change takes place, this army must inevitably be reduced to one or the other of these three things: starve, dissolve, or disperse."[18]

Two questions leap out from our unpainted picture: first, why was the Continental Army undergoing a near-death experience in some previously obscure region of southeastern Pennsylvania; second, what did Washington mean by "capital change"? The answer to both questions is almost designed to prove disorienting to most modern-day Americans, who carry assumptions about the patriotic orientation of the revolutionary generation that misconstrue the political mentality of that lost world. Moreover, the recovery of that lost world exposes the confining political parameters that rendered any national resolution of the slavery question virtually impossible throughout the war years and beyond.

For example, the first sentence of the most famous speech in American history is factually incorrect. Abraham Lincoln began his remarks at Gettysburg in 1863 as follows: "Four score and seven years ago"—that is, in 1776—"our fathers brought forth, on this continent, a new nation." Not really. The resolution declaring independence approved on July 2, 1776, clearly stated that the former colonies were leaving the British Empire as "free and independent States," not as an independent nation-state. Loyalties throughout the thirteen former colonies remained local; the political horizons of the ordinary citizens were confined to the fences around their farms; they could not think nationally.[19]

Only a month before the "Cavalcade of Wild Beasts" marched into Valley Forge, the Continental Congress approved final revisions of the aforementioned Dickinson Draft, outlining the shape of a new federal government entitled the Articles of Confederation. It created a state-based framework virtually identical to the government proposed by the Confederacy in 1861. (Small wonder that Lincoln was forced to falsify history to justify his opposition to southern secession.) The deplorable conditions of the Continental Army at Valley Forge were actually reassuring to many otherwise patriotic Americans, who regarded it as a domestic version of the British army, which they were supposedly rebelling against.[20]

By "capital change" Washington meant a truly major shift from a deliberately weak central government in which sovereignty resided in the states to a federal government empowered to make domestic and foreign policy for an emerging American nation. As he put it, "Unless Congress have powers competent to all general purposes, the distresses we have encountered, the expense we have incurred, and the blood we have spilt will avail us nothing."

Though his national vision would bear fruit ten years later at the Constitutional Convention, at Valley Forge he was speaking into the wind, and only his fellow sufferers in the snow within the offi- cer corps were listening. For the vast majority of the civilian popu- lation, the term "United States" was a plural noun; "union" referred to a temporary and provisional allegiance of sovereign states free to go their separate ways when the war was won; and a fully empow- ered federal government embodied all the tyrannical tendencies of the loathsome British leviathan itself.[21]

Given the state-based structure of the Articles, no national ini- tiative to put slavery on the road to extinction could occur, since no federal government empowered to impose its will on the states existed. Fifty years later, during the antebellum era, when a south- ern statesman pontificated on the hallowed principle of states' rights, one could be reasonably sure that he was delivering a thinly disguised defense of slavery. That was not the case, however, dur- ing the war for independence or immediately thereafter. During those decades, state sovereignty was a heartfelt conviction with deep roots in the population-at-large in both northern and south- ern states. It had nothing directly to do with slavery and everything to do with a bottom-up version of patriotism that was deeply sus- picious of any political power that originated beyond the limited range of its own local horizons. Think of it as a principled commit- ment to provincialism.[22]

o o o

As a result, the first chapter in what American historians call the Abolitionist Movement began at the state level during the war for independence in five northern states: Vermont (still an aspir- ing state), Massachusetts, Pennsylvania, Connecticut, and Rhode Island. In every state, the core values of The Cause as articulated in the Declaration of Independence, often reiterated in the same uplifting Jeffersonian language, became the rationale for either ending slavery in the state constitutions outright or doing so gradually. The Vermont Constitution, for example, proclaimed "that all persons are born equally free and independent, and have certain natural, inherent, and inalienable rights, amongst which are the enjoying and defending life and liberty. . . ." Although every state was different, and needed to tell its own story in its own distinctive way, the unifying thread that bound them all together was the values they had proclaimed to the world as the rationale for leaving the British Empire, which were inherently and self-evidently incompatible with slavery.[23]

One southern state, all-important Virginia, took a step in the same direction, then backed away. The Virginia Constitution, drafted by George Mason, contained the same expansive language about human rights as Jefferson's Declaration. (As we know, Jefferson had copied from Mason's draft to write "pursuit of happiness.") But during the debate in the Virginia legislature, several prominent planters demanded the insertion of a phrase limiting those natural rights proclaimed by Mason to "those who enter into a state of society." This amended language excluded African Americans and Native Americans from the social contract, a clever, lawyerlike way to take slavery off the agenda in the Old Dominion.[24]

Although the debate over slavery in Pennsylvania was driven by the same principled commitment to the egalitarian values of The Cause, it took place in the Pennsylvania Assembly rather than the courts. As a result, political compromises between the Quaker elite in Philadelphia and adamantly opposed slaveholders in rural regions of the state proved unavoidable, which in turn meant that the nonnegotiable moral principles of The Cause were forced to negotiate with the political realities of a divided electorate of white voters. It was one thing to declare that "those who contend for their own freedom are compelled to promote the liberty of others" at a

Quaker meeting. It was quite another to win a statewide election with the same moralistic agenda remaining intact.[25]

From the very start of the debate in Pennsylvania, immediate emancipation, as had occurred in Vermont and Massachusetts, was off the table, and some form of gradual emancipation was the only realistic option. After much backing and forthing behind closed doors, the final draft of the bill ending slavery in Pennsylvania deferred emancipation into the future, when children born of enslaved mothers reached twenty-eight years of age. It did not liberate anyone currently enslaved, or deprive current slaveholders of their enslaved property. Without these concessions, the law ending slavery in Pennsylvania would not have passed. It did so on March 1, 1780, by a vote of thirty-four to twenty-one.[26]

The debate over slavery in Pennsylvania established a framework for gradual emancipation subsequently adopted by Connecticut and Rhode Island, and then, after a long wait, in New York and New Jersey. The debate in Pennsylvania exposed the inherent conflict between the moral certainties at the core of The Cause and the political realities facing any plan for emancipation dependent upon a popular referendum of white voters. What worked in Quaker meetings and New Light congregations did not work in legislatures. Pennsylvania thereby provided a preview of the irreconcilable split between moralists and pragmatists in the emerging Abolitionist Movement throughout the founding era.

As long as the war was ongoing, the pragmatists enjoyed the upper hand, for the simple reason that winning the war required a united front, so the pressure for both sides to meet in the middle was enormous; and slavery, more than any other issue, possessed the potential to blow up the provisional union essential for victory in the war. But there was also a clear sectional split beneath the surface. In the northern states, compromise meant gradual emancipation. In the southern states, it meant postponing the argument with their northern brethren for the duration of the war. Both sides, in fact, agreed that the slavery question should be deferred. But in the north that meant until after the war; in the south it meant until hell froze over.

∘ ∘ ∘

For the first five years of the war, from 1775 to 1780, all the major engagements occurred north of the Potomac—in Canada, Massachusetts, New York, New Jersey, and Pennsylvania. This effectively meant that more than four hundred thousand enslaved African Americans in Virginia, the Carolinas, and Georgia were isolated bystanders; and the main mission of militia units in each of the southern states was to patrol their counties in order to discourage runaways and any putative slave insurrections, which, partly for that reason, never occurred. The Dunmore episode had exposed the latent urge to escape bondage, which did not require a reading of Jefferson's lyrical tribute to human equality for inspiration. Like a beautiful vista's beauty, it was simply there. But until the war moved to the southern theater, it had nowhere to go.

That changed in 1780, because of a fundamental shift in British strategy. The triggering event was French entry into the war in 1778, which prompted a full-scale reappraisal of British strategic priorities. "The object of the war being now changed," Lord George Germain wrote to General Henry Clinton, "and the conflict in America being a secondary consideration, our principal object must be distressing France and defending His Majesty's possessions elsewhere." The epicenter of "elsewhere" was the Caribbean, most especially Jamaica, which provided more revenue to the empire than all the American colonies put together.[27]

It was ironic: A major rationale for the British decision to oppose American independence was the fear that it would set off a chain reaction in the other British colonies, an early version of the "domino theory." Now, however, French entry into the war revealed that the dominoes could fall in the other direction. For, if the British devoted the bulk of their naval and land forces to the American theater, they risked losing Jamaica, Barbados, and perhaps even India to their most serious rival for European supremacy.

What became a southern strategy that eventually put the huge enslaved population from Virginia to Georgia into play began as something quite different: namely, a plan to make Charleston the platform for the British fleet during the hurricane season in the Caribbean. It did not look that way to Washington, whose spies in New York apprised him that General Henry Clinton, who had succeeded William Howe as commander of His Majesty's forces in North America, was assembling an invasion force of nine thousand troops to attack and capture Charleston, which was defended by an American garrison of five thousand troops, a majority of whom were militia.

As Washington saw it, there was little he could do to reinforce the garrison in Charleston. He lacked a fleet to transport troops, and had few men to spare anyway. Sending a token force over-land to South Carolina would prove meaningless, like firing a cannonball into outer space. At this point, one of his young aides, John Laurens, stepped forward with a not-so-modest proposal. He would return to South Carolina, his home state, and raise an all-black regiment of three thousand enslaved African Americans, who would be offered freedom in return for service in defending Charleston.[28]

If The Cause was a religion, Laurens was an evangelical. "I have long deplored the wretched state of these men" (i.e., slaves), he explained to his father, Henry Laurens, one of the wealthi-est planters in South Carolina, "and consider in their history the bloody wars excited in Africa to furnish America with slaves, the horror of a despairing multitude toiling for the Luxuries of Merci-less Tyrants." His closest friend, Alexander Hamilton, an equally young member of Washington's staff, strongly endorsed the Laurens initiative. "An essential part of the plan," he explained, "is to give them their freedom with their muskets. This will assure their fidelity, animate their courage, and have a good influence upon those who remain, by opening a door to their emancipation." Although he expressed some reservations, Washington endorsed the Laurens proposal, as did the Continental Congress. Never one to dally, Laurens galloped south to make his case to the South Carolina legislature.[29]

As his father had warned him, when Laurens made his proposal to the legislature, he was greeted with some combination of incredulity, outrage, and the widespread sense that the younger Laurens had lost his mind. Laurens responded in kind, later apprising Washington, "The single voice of reason was drowned out by the howling of a triple-headed monster in which Prejudice, Avarice, and Pusillanimity were united."[30]

Rather than undergo a long and destructive siege, Governor John Rutledge drafted terms of surrender, whereby South Carolina would accept British occupation for the remainder of the war, thereby "deferring the question whether it belonged to Great Britain or the United States until conclusion of the war, accepting whatever was granted to the other states." In effect, when asked to choose between independence and slavery, South Carolina chose slavery. But the siege occurred anyway, because Clinton refused to permit the troops in the Charleston garrison to be released on their own recognizance. The British bombardment destroyed most of the city. The white flag went up on May 12, 1780. This was the most costly American defeat in the war, with fifty-five hundred troops taken prisoner, including a wounded Laurens.[31]

British strategy for the southern theater shifted dramatically in response to reliable rumors from several European capitals. Diplomats in Paris, Madrid, Vienna, and St. Petersburg announced plans for an intervention to end the fighting on the grounds that the war had gone on too long and was disrupting all the European economies. (It was a characteristic of the Eurocentric mentality to presume that its own interests were hegemonic.) If and when the armistice went into effect, the doctrine of *uti possidetis*, roughly translated as "keep what you own," would freeze the contested regions of North America based on military control when the fighting ceased. This in turn meant that, if Charles Cornwallis, now commanding the British army after General Clinton returned to New York, could roam about the Carolinas, Georgia, and perhaps even Virginia unopposed, Great Britain could claim possession of all the land south of the Potomac.

This new strategy fit nicely with Cornwallis's own aggressive instincts, and with reports in the London press describing him as the newly arrived British Hannibal. (Just as Hannibal performed a military miracle by crossing the Alps with his elephants, Cornwallis was expected to perform a comparable miracle by conquering a contested region larger than France with four thousand troops.) In response to the same European rumors, Washington dispatched his most trusted general, Nathanael Greene, to oppose Cornwallis and thereby claim American control of the southern theater. All of a sudden, and for the first time in the war, the enslaved population in the Carolinas and Georgia was almost inadvertently put into play. In response to a vaguely worded proclamation by General Clinton that echoed the earlier promises of Lord Dunmore, a veritable flood of enslaved African Americans, most traveling in family units, fled their plantations by the thousands. And they kept coming.[32]

What were they thinking? The short answer is: we do not know. Several former slaves who reached freedom by serving in the Continental Army left a written record of their reasoning. Here, for example, is Prince Whipple, a New Hampshire slave explaining himself to the state legislature: "We know that we ought to be free agents. Here we feel the dignity of human nature. Here we feel the passions and desires of men, un-checked by the rod of slavery."[33]

Nothing comparable exists for the much larger runaway population in the southern states, where eloquence was apparently unnecessary, where The Cause emerged from a more primal level inside their souls beyond the refinement imposed by words. In one sense, it was the purest form of The Cause, for its truths truly were self-evident.

Within weeks, more than ten thousand escaped slaves were on their way toward the promised land. Only about half that number made it to Cornwallis's army. The remainder were captured by local militia units, bands of privateers, or swallowed up in the wartime confusion generated by multiple gangs of terrorists posing as patriots or loyalists. Cornwallis himself observed that the inherent chaos throughout the Carolina countryside took him by surprise: "Without restraints the war in this quarter will become truly savage." It already was.[34]

Although Cornwallis was commanding a tiny army, reduced to two thousand troops after heavy losses at Cowpens and Guilford Court House, he never gave any consideration to forming an all-black regiment or integrating the male runaways into his combat units. He was willing to employ several hundred Blacks as laborers, driving wagons or pulling artillery pieces, but came to regard the remaining runaways, especially the women and children, as burdens that slowed down his pursuit of Greene's army.

With Clinton's permission, he ordered all escaped slaves owned by loyalists returned to their plantations. His major policy change was the creation of "sequestered estates," devastated plantations where he sent nearly five thousand former slaves to provide food and livestock for his regulars. The runaways that kept arriving he regarded as excess baggage. He made no effort to inoculate them, and they proceeded to die in droves within weeks.[35]

The fullest description of his army on the march comes from Johann Ewald, a Hessian officer serving with Cornwallis. It resembled, wrote Ewald, "a wandering Arabian or Tartar horde that descended like locusts on every acre of farmland it passed. Every officer had four to six horses and three or four Negroes, as well as one or two Negresses for cook and maid. Every soldier had his Negro, who carried his provisions and bundles." Cornwallis had agreed to requests from his senior officers to distribute his otherwise burdensome black baggage among the troops as their personal slaves, which gave his army on the march the appearance of a plantation on the move.[36]

Here is another one of those unpainted scenes worthy of our recovery. But historical accuracy requires that we identify the location as Virginia, not South Carolina, and perhaps mention that seventeen of the enslaved entourage came from Mount Vernon and twenty-three from Monticello. The obvious question poses itself: why was Cornwallis in Virginia? The short answer is that he was ordered to invade Virginia by his superiors in London, who were harboring the illusion that Cornwallis had established British control over the Carolinas and should now carry the momentum of the southern campaign into Virginia. The longer answer is that Cornwallis was fully aware that his campaign in the Carolinas had failed, but for that very reason was eager to embrace the order to invade Virginia, which would be the most valuable piece on the American chessboard if and when the doctrine of "keep what you control" became the guiding principle in a negotiated settlement.[37]

Virginia had good reason to believe that it, not Pennsylvania, deserved to be called the Keystone State. Geographically, it was the largest state. Demographically, it contained the largest population, which was bolstered by 220,000 enslaved Blacks. Less palpably, the most prominent planters carried a presumptive sense of their significance. (As John Adams liked to joke, in Virginia all geese were swans.) The fact that the British army and navy had ignored Virginia for the first five years of the war almost seemed an insult.

This neglect ended three months before Cornwallis brought his badly shredded army up from the Carolinas, when Clinton dispatched the American traitor Benedict Arnold, with sixteen hundred mostly Hessian troops, to seize the harbor at Portsmouth, then conduct raiding parties inland in order to disrupt the supply line to Greene's army in South Carolina. Arnold, the most hated man in America, destined to become the greatest traitor in American history, expanded his mandate by attacking the new Virginia capital at Richmond, burning much of it to the ground, then marching through the Tidewater region in a scorched-earth campaign that even his subordinate officers found excessively vengeful. Arnold clearly believed he had something to prove. What he unintentionally proved was that Virginia's enslaved population, without options since Dunmore's departure, was poised for a breakout. They fled to Arnold's army by the thousands.[38]

Virginia's governor at the time was Thomas Jefferson, who was facing considerable criticism for permitting the Old Dominion to become so vulnerable to the unexpected British invasion. Writing from his headquarters outside New York, Washington offered some semblance of help by sending the Marquis de Lafayette south with twelve hundred troops. "From the most recent European intelligence," Washington wrote to Jefferson, "the British are seeking to make conquests [in Virginia] that then may enlarge the plea of *uti possitetis* [sic] in the proposed mediation." And without Virginia, an independent America made little geographic sense. Given the stakes, Lafayette's small force was obviously inadequate, but all Washington could spare.[39]

One obvious answer would have been the mobilization of the huge enslaved population, but the delegates in the Virginia legislature dismissed that option with the same resounding horror that their colleagues in South Carolina had a year earlier. Instead, they authorized bonuses to attract white recruits payable in specie or "one healthy black between the ages of ten and thirty." Blacks could be bartered as slaves, but not freed as soldiers. Small wonder virtually all the runaways in Virginia recognized that the British army was their only realistic destination.[40]

When Cornwallis entered Virginia, he inherited a sizable force that expanded his army to seven thousand troops, soon trailed by a parade of four thousand former slaves that kept increasing with newly arrived runaways, but at a slower rate because of death by disease, mostly smallpox. Cornwallis took his multicolored caravan inland as far as Petersburg in pursuit of Lafayette's token force.

Otherwise, the British army moved at will through the Old Dominion, once again devastating Richmond, destroying the entire tobacco crop for the season, almost capturing Jefferson at his beloved Monticello, and generating a robust correspondence among the most prominent Virginians about who lost the most slaves to the intruders. Jefferson later estimated that three thousand slaves fled to the British army in Virginia, a number that earlier historians thought too high, but more recently find too low.

Whatever the correct number, there was clearly a large collection of African American runaways available for military service and for British-inspired slave insurrections, in effect for a potentially devastating "southern strategy" that might very well have altered the outcome of the war. But neither the British ministry nor Cornwallis embraced such a strategy.[41]

o o o

Cornwallis was forced to end his campaign to secure British control of the Virginia interior when he received an order from Clinton to move his army to the coastline, specifically the harbor at Yorktown. Clinton believed that the Continental Army, with French support, was poised to attack New York, and therefore he needed a portion of Cornwallis's army to bolster its defense. Cornwallis loathed Clinton, and defending an entrenched position was not in his repertoire, but this time he obeyed the order, presuming that the coastline location assured the protection of the British navy.

But it did not. On August 30, 1781, a huge French fleet of twenty-eight ships led by Admiral de Grasse appeared at the mouth of the Chesapeake. A week later, it soundly defeated a somewhat smaller British fleet in the Battle of the Chesapeake, the largest naval engagement of the war in the Atlantic theater. Only a few days later, a combined Franco-American force, under the joint command of George Washington and Count Rochambeau, totaling nearly forty thousand soldiers and sailors, arrived just in time to view the British sails on the horizon, limping back to New York. "What may be in the Womb of Fate is very uncertain," Washington wrote upon his arrival, "but we anticipate the reduction of Cornwallis and his entire army."[42]

By early October, Cornwallis's situation had become hopeless. It happened that Rochambeau was a proven master of siege warfare, and his military engineers were renowned as the best in Europe. Once they dug their angled trenches, then moved their heavy artillery into point-blank range, death rained down on the helpless British defenders all day and night. Cornwallis moved his headquarters into a cave. The three thousand former slaves—down from four thousand because of smallpox—remained vulnerable to shrapnel in their makeshift trenches, suffering thirty to forty casualties a day.

Meanwhile, on the other side of the battlefield, Washington selected the predominantly African American Rhode Island regiment to lead the assault on a heavily defended redoubt that needed to be taken to complete the last row of siege trenches. Hamilton persuaded Washington to let him lead the nighttime attack, then recruited his closest friend, John Laurens, to join him in risking their lives with black troops, whose cause they had both championed.* Hamilton vaulted into the redoubt on the back of a black sergeant, another one of those unpainted scenes that deserve to be remembered—the epitome of a biracial version of The Cause.[43]

As his casualties mounted, and it became clear that rescue by the British fleet, currently undergoing repairs in New York, would not occur in time to avoid near annihilation, Cornwallis made a desperate attempt to liberate a portion of his beleaguered army in a late-night dash across the York River to Gloucester Point. But a sudden storm capsized the small ships carrying his designated survivors. The luck was evenly divided at Yorktown: the British got all the bad, the Americans all the good.

Just before he sent up the white flag, Cornwallis expelled all his black support troops infected with smallpox and their respective families. (Whether he thought he was freeing them or abandoning them is unclear.) Private Joseph Plumb Martin described the scene in his memoir, published fifty years later as *Private Yankee Doodle:*

> During the siege, we saw in the woods herds of Negroes, which Lord Cornwallis, after he had inveigled them from their proprietors, in love and pity to them, had turned adrift, with no other recompense for their confidence in his humanity than smallpox for their bounty and starvation and death for their wages. They might be seen scattered about in every direction, dead and dying, with pieces of burnt Indian corn in their hands and mouths, even those that were dead.

The scene Martin described is almost an exact replica of the unpainted picture from five years earlier, the scene of Dunmore's dying followers on an island not far from Yorktown. Taken together,

---

* Laurens, who had been in British captivity, had only recently recovered from the wounds suffered at Charleston and been exchanged for a British officer of equivalent rank.

these images remind us that viruses, not bombs and bullets, were the weapons of mass destruction during the war for independence, in fact would remain so in all wars until the discovery of antibiotics in the early twentieth century.* But disease, especially smallpox, had a lethal impact on the population of escaped slaves throughout the war, killing more runaways than ever found their way into the historical record, making it virtually impossible to know with any accuracy how many enslaved African Americans opted to defy the odds and flee.[44]

The best guess is that several hundred escaped slaves survived the smallpox epidemic and the battlefield carnage at Yorktown. Washington had insisted on the insertion of a clause in the Articles of Capitulation that these survivors must be recaptured: "It is understood that any property obviously belonging to the inhabitants of these states, in the possession of the garrison, shall be subject to be reclaimed." Although the war had been an educational experience for Washington on the slavery issue, when it came to his own slaves, he was still thinking like a typical Virginia slaveowner. He had lost seventeen of his Mount Vernon slaves to the British, and he wanted them back.[45]

He was not numb to the larger moral issues at stake, but such concerns still floated above the palpable and almost primal conviction that his slaves belonged to him. In fact, Washington only recovered two of his former slaves. And he chose to look away when Cornwallis requested that the *Bonetta* sail "without examination," allegedly to apprise Clinton of the capitulation, knowing full well that it contained many loyalists and escaped slaves, including some of his own. He apparently did not wish to appear to be acting in his own self-interest.

Great Britain was accustomed to winning wars, but did not know

---

* The runaways from Mount Vernon were able to beat the odds, because Washington had ordered all his slaves inoculated.

how to lose. The surrender ceremony at Yorktown captured that confusion. Cornwallis refused to show up, pleading illness. When marching between the French and American lines, many British soldiers were crying, others shouting obscenities at the smiling Americans. One Hessian officer wondered out loud at the improbability of losing to a group of unshaven, often shoeless hooligans. The only American troops who looked like soldiers, he observed, were the mostly black members of the Rhode Island regiment.[46]

Three months later, in January 1782, Cornwallis, a recently exchanged prisoner of war, declared to assembled reporters in London that "the conquest of America by fire and sword is not to be accomplished, let your numbers be what they may." In effect, the war against the Americans was inherently unwinnable, always had been, and always would be if the British ministry insisted on protracting the conflict.[47] Admiral Samuel Graves also provided a naval metaphor for the British strategic dilemma: "The movement of the British army through the American landscape was like the passage of a ship through the sea, whose track is soon lost to the waves." The British army needed not only to win battles but to control the terrain after the battles were won, to become both an army of conquest and an army of occupation. It was never large enough to accomplish both missions.[48]

The huge potential manpower source of the enslaved population could have been mobilized to create several black regiments. But, as we have seen, there was a long-standing prejudice against allowing Blacks to serve alongside Whites in British combat units. Whether an enlarged, more biracial British force would have made a decisive difference is impossible to know.

○ ○ ○

The prominent American exchanged for Cornwallis was Henry Laurens, who had been captured at sea on his way to join the

American negotiating team in Paris as the designated representative of the southern states. While imprisoned in the Tower of London on the charge of treason, Laurens learned that his famous son, John, had gone down in a meaningless engagement outside of Savannah. (No surprise: Young Laurens rejected orders to wait for reinforcements, then led a cavalry charge against entrenched British troops. Hit in the heart, he was dead before he hit the ground.) The loudest southern voice for making The Cause synonymous with emancipation was silenced forever.[49]

Once freed, Henry Laurens made his way to Versailles, joining the diplomatic team of Benjamin Franklin, John Adams, and John Jay as the negotiations were nearing an end. He was just in time to insert a stipulation that "British troops should carry off no Negroes or other American property when departing." The provision must have sent his son rolling over in his grave. But, as the only member of the American delegation from a southern state, Henry Laurens apparently felt obliged to represent the economic interest of the planter class. Whatever his motives, Laurens's words in the provisional treaty ending the war created a moral dilemma for officers overseeing the British evacuation in 1783.[50]

The sheer scale of the British evacuation posed massive logistical challenges that required the largest amphibious operation in British naval history: over four hundred ships to transport twenty thousand troops, thirty thousand loyalists, and twenty thousand former slaves from New York, Charleston, and Savannah, the only patches of ground the British controlled after seven years of costly war. Two British officers were assigned the monumental mission of managing the evacuation: General Guy Carleton, the only senior British officer who could claim that he had won his piece of the war by repelling all American efforts to capture Quebec, thereby assuring that Canada would remain a British colony; and General Alexander Leslie, a seven-year veteran of the war, whom Corn-

wallis had dispatched to Charleston shortly before the trap closed
around his army at Yorktown.

The logistical challenges were amplified by the political dilemma posed by the last-minute entry in the provisional treaty
requiring Great Britain to return all escaped slaves in their possession to their American owners. Leslie led the way in claiming that
they had a professional obligation as British officers to disregard
the treaty. "Those who have voluntarily come in under the faith of
our protection," he wrote to Carleton, "cannot in justice be abandoned to the merciless prejudices of their former masters." Carleton
concurred, even though he was being badgered by a steady stream
of slaveowners and their agents, demanding the recovery of their
most valuable property.[51]

The most prominent petitioner of all was George Washington,
who requested one of his agents to plead his case: "Some of my
own slaves may probably be in New York," he explained, "and if by
chance you should come by the knowledge of any of them, I will
be much obliged to you for securing them, so I may obtain them
again."[52]

At a face-to-face meeting, Carleton apprised Washington that
four Mount Vernon slaves had already been evacuated to Nova
Scotia, and there was no way to have them recalled, since they
now were free men and women. When asked by what authority he
could overrule the treaty requiring him to return all escaped slaves,
Carleton cited his authority as British commander on the scene,
and his confidence that posterity would almost surely endorse his
judgment. Washington walked away convinced that future negotiations were futile. He advised Benjamin Harrison, the governor
of Virginia, to drop the subject, since there was "little expectation
that any of these characters will be returned," and that he himself
had "little enthusiasm for it." When several prominent Virginia
planters asked him to sign a petition protesting British violations

of the peace treaty, Washington refused. When the requests kept coming, he did not respond. He did not want his name associated with any scheme to recover lost slaves.[53]

He was no longer the typical Virginia squire who could afford to think of his slaves as if they were cows or pigs, though his old instincts along those lines still vibrated. He had become a legend-in-the-making, for whom Carleton's reference to posterity's judgment had begun to assume a newfound significance. While not yet prepared to stake out a leadership position on the slavery issue, he did sense where history was headed on that crucial question, and he did not want his legacy enshrined on the wrong side in the minds of future generations. He could not lead, but he would not follow the lead of other Virginia slaveowners.[54]

Despite their best intentions, neither Carleton nor Leslie could control the fate of nearly ten thousand escaped slaves owned by loyalists, who were destined to remain slaves wherever their owners were sent. Slightly more than a thousand ended up in Quebec or New Brunswick, in eastern Canada. The much larger group, sailing out of Charleston and Savannah, were temporarily relocated to East Florida, then moved to the Bahamas or, the unlucky ones, to Jamaica.

Most of the ten thousand runaways owned by members of the resistance reached the promised land in Nova Scotia or England. The evacuation to Nova Scotia was a well-organized migration of about five thousand men, women, and children sailing out of New York. The evacuation to England was a disorganized, impromptu affair led by British officers who insisted on taking their long-standing servants with them, and stowaways were permitted aboard by ship captains who looked the other way. Once in England, all escaped slaves were declared free under British law. An unknowable number of former slaves transported from Charleston or Savannah to New York fled to the free black community there, and eventually disappeared into similar locations in Philadelphia and Boston.[55]

The best estimate, then, is that almost half the twenty thousand runaways in British hands during the evacuation reached freedom. Though this was only half the proverbial loaf, given the inherently chaotic character of the evacuation process that all losers in foreign wars seem to encounter, it can and should be regarded as a major achievement, rendered possible by two British officers determined to place honor above duty.

It is more difficult to know the size of the runaway population that never made it to the evacuation sites, primarily because they disappeared in multiple ways that never found a way into the record books. As noted earlier, some were captured by militia only a few miles from their plantations. Some were scooped up by roving bands of privateers for sale to slaveowners in the Caribbean. But by far the greatest number died of disease, primarily smallpox and typhus.

Though all estimates are educated guesses, it is safe to say that the road to freedom was a gauntlet that claimed many more lives than those who survived to reach the evacuation sites. More African Americans lost their lives pursuing their distinctive version of The Cause than the official casualty lists for the war have counted. A memorial to "Many Thousands Gone" at Arlington Cemetery is long overdue.[56]

○ ○ ○

The most immediate and historically significant postwar event occurred on December 23, 1783, at Annapolis, Maryland, where Washington appeared to surrender his commission. He concluded his address to the Confederation Congress with the following words: "Having now finished the work assigned me, I retire from the great theater of action, and bidding farewell to the august body under whom I have long acted, I offer here my commission and take leave of all the employment of public life." It was the greatest exit, and perhaps the most consequential moment, in American history.[57]

Thomas Jefferson, who was present in the audience, understood what he had just witnessed. "The moderation and character of a single man," he wrote a friend, "has probably prevented the revolution from being closed as most others have been, by a subversion of the liberty it was intended to establish." Jefferson was thinking of the precedents set by Caesar and Cromwell. If he had had access to a crystal ball, he would have conjured up Napoleon, Lenin, Stalin, Mao, Castro, and a host of African dictators.[58]

Washington's resignation was reported with awe and amazement in European newspapers from London to Vienna. When word reached George III, he found it difficult to believe. If it was true, he declared, "he will become the greatest man in the world." In fact, the world was witnessing a new definition of political leadership, rooted in the ability to surrender rather than exercise power. It was unprecedented. And it meant that the Americans were serious about becoming the first nation-sized republic since Rome.[59]

But all the political energies in play were moving in the opposite direction. The government created near the end of the war, called the Articles of Confederation, was a loose union of sovereign states that had come together to win the war and were now returning to their prewar status as independent republics of their own. All the political waters were receding to the state and local level. Any national government empowered to make domestic and foreign policy was stigmatized as the second coming of Parliament. Alexander Hamilton offered his regretful but realistic assessment of the postwar political context:

> We have now happily concluded the great work of independence, but much remains to be done to reach the fruits of it. Our prospects are not flattering. Every day proves the inefficiency of the present confederation, yet the common danger

being removed, we are receding instead of advancing in a disposition to amend its defects. It is hoped that when prejudice and folly run themselves out of breath we may return to reason and correct our errors.[60]

As far as progress on the slavery question was concerned, the timing could not have been worse. For when the antislavery implications of The Cause were still simmering, if not burning brightly, the state-based structure of the Articles rendered any emancipation proposal at the national level impossible. Such an initiative could only come from the states.

Predictably, the egalitarian implications of The Cause continued to gain traction in all the northern states except New York and New Jersey, where the size of the enslaved population was largest. At first glance, the southern states, where the vast majority of the enslaved population resided, looked like another country immune to the values of The Cause, or prepared to live with the contradiction.

On closer examination, however, there was a discernible split between the upper and lower south, most visibly exposed in the different postures of Virginia and South Carolina. In the Old Dominion, The Cause was still throbbing away, as revealed in the decision in 1782 to permit owners to free their slaves on their own. Such a policy was unimaginable in both South Carolina and Georgia, where, as one prominent planter put it, "Slavery is to the life of this country as the Soul is to the Body." The deeper the southern accent, the deeper the commitment to slavery.[61]

If a well-informed observer had been standing on the cusp of the moment after the war ended, he might with confidence have foreseen the following developments: George Washington would embrace his role as the American Cincinnatus and remain retired at Mount Vernon until called to the hereafter; the renamed American Union, a forerunner of the European Union, would allow the antislavery north to coexist peacefully with the proslavery south, thereby demonstrating that a house divided against itself could stand; under the leadership of the famed Virginia Dynasty, the Old Dominion would declare itself neutral on the slavery question, thereby providing an invaluable link between the two sections; the steadily growing slave population, lacking the available destination provided by the British army, would gradually adjust to its condition, and the threat of slave insurrections would become a distant memory.

On all accounts, he would have been wrong.

Chapter 5

The Ghost at the Banquet

º º º

I am afraid you will think this project, if not extravagant,
absolutely unattainable and unworthy of being attempted.
—JAMES MADISON to Edmund Randolph, April 8, 1787

THERE IS A consensus among historians that the Treaty
of Paris (1783), though coming at the very start, can be
regarded as the greatest triumph in the annals of American diplomacy. Its two cardinal achievements were the recognition
of American independence and the acquisition of the eastern third
of the North American continent—all the land south of Canada,
north of Florida, and east of the Mississippi—a landmass larger
than England, France, and Spain put together.

When Benjamin West, the American-born artist and favorite of
George III, accepted a commission to paint the negotiators of the
treaty, the British delegation refused to show up, fearful of being
memorialized for posterity as the losers of Britain's North American empire to an upstart American empire of its own.[1]

When George Washington sat down to write his last Circular
Letter to the States, in June 1783, he was uncharacteristically eloquent about the acquisition of a vast western domain:

The Citizens of America, placed in the most enviable condition, as the sole Lords and Proprietors of a vast Tract of Continent, comprehending all the various soils and climates of the World, and abounding with all the necessaries and conveniences of life, are now by the late satisfactory pacification, acknowledged to be possessed of absolute freedom and Independency; they are, from this period, to be considered as Actors on a most conspicuous Theatre, which seems to be peculiarly designated by Providence for the display of human greatness and felicity. . . .[2]

Over a century before Frederick Jackson Turner made western expansion the central theme in American history, Washington realized that the occupation and settlement of the not-so vacant land to the west would define America's domestic agenda for generations to come. Europe was the past. The American west was the future.[3]

Moreover, at least as Washington saw it, those western horizons fundamentally changed the chemistry of the political conversation by rendering the local and state perspectives of the current confederation pathetically provincial and mindlessly myopic. Throughout the war, the states had been held together, however tentatively, by the common goal of independence. But once that goal was achieved, the states were poised to go their separate ways, loosely confederated under the Articles. Now, in Washington's view, the west replaced the war as the common bond. How to manage this extraordinary asset was obviously the central question facing the next generation of American political leaders, and doing so would require them to think nationally rather than locally.

There were two glaring omissions in this otherwise uplifting vision: first, the presence of an indigenous population whose rights to their ancestral lands could not be ignored without violating the consensual values of The Cause; second, the sectional split between northern and southern states over slavery, already quite discernible, which rendered conflict over the incoming territories more than likely.*

Although the Articles of Confederation were designed to be weak, one power they did possess was to define the terms for the admission of territories as states. The first occasion to exercise that power occurred in 1784, shortly after the Virginia delegation ceded its claims to the vast expanse of land northwest of the Ohio River. The Virginia delegation proposed the following principles: "The Territories so ceded shall be laid out and formed into states . . . and . . . the states so formed shall be distinctive Republican states and admitted as members of the Federal Union, having the same rights of Sovereignty, Freedom, and Independence as the other states." The words were written by Thomas Jefferson, and it is possible to argue that, apart from his more famous phrases in the Declaration of Independence, they are the most historically consequential words he ever wrote, since they defined the political and legal framework that would shape American expansion across the North American continent for the next century, a framework that was itself shaped by the core principles of The Cause.[4]

Those principles became more explicit in the Ordinance of 1784, also drafted by Jefferson. None of the territories could become colonies; all must be admitted to the union as republics on equal terms with other states. All hereditary titles would be repudiated. And, most important, slavery would end no later than 1800. The entire course of American history might have changed if the stipulation on slavery had won acceptance in the Confederation Congress, but it lost by one vote.[5]

o o o

---

* Washington can be excused for lacking a crystal ball, but our hindsight wisdom permits us to know that, when the southern states seceded in 1861, the triggering issue was Lincoln's policy to exclude slavery in all incoming territories.

Jefferson's role during the debate on the Ordinance of 1784 proved to be the high point of his commitment to ending slavery. It also proved to be the last occasion when the egalitarian implications of The Cause retained their political prowess as what Abraham Lincoln later called "the better angels of our Nature." What we are witnessing was the start of a new chapter in the American founding—indeed, the launching of what might justifiably be called the "Great Debate" in American political history. The issue at stake was whether the infant American republic should remain a confederation of sovereign states or become a full-fledged nation-state.

Our perch in the present provides some semblance of omniscience, knowing as we do that the Great Debate would culminate at the Constitutional Convention, then the ratification debates in twelve of the thirteen states, then the passing of what would come to be called the Bill of Rights. Unfortunately, our omniscience also blinds us to the unorthodox and decidedly desperate way that history happened. The vast majority of ordinary Americans were completely comfortable with the inherent weakness of the Articles of Confederation—in fact, regarded its weakness as its greatest strength.

Nor could the Articles be revised from within, since all efforts to do so would be blocked by the very state-based framework that needed revising.

Since any movement to revise or replace the Articles could not bubble up from below, or come from within, it could only happen from the top down, led by a small group of nationalists willing and able to defy popular opinion. Though this sounds almost un-American, it had to be a coup d'état, led by prominent figures united in their conviction that the full promise of the American Revolution could only be realized within the political framework of a national government. The trio of co-conspirators consisted of John Jay, Alexander Hamilton, and James Madison.[6]

Jay came to the task as secretary of foreign affairs, a reward for his brilliant service in negotiating the Treaty of Paris. His first act was to send a letter to all the governors, requesting them to forward all correspondence relating to foreign policy to his office. Few of the governors responded, none complied, and all the states presumed they could make their own foreign policy. Writing from London, Abigail Adams complained that she and her husband represented a government that did not exist. Jay empathized, writing John Adams that "our federal government is incompetent to its objects," then declaring that he did not just want the Articles reformed, he wanted them replaced: "It is my first wish to see the United States assume the merit and character of one great nation. Until this was done, the chain which holds us together will be too feeble to bear much opposition and we shall be easily mortified by seeing the links of it give way."[7]

Hamilton shared Jay's disappointment with the inadequacies of the Articles, but his chief focus was their failure to address the mounting debt, and the aggressive Hamilton style, appropriate for storming a redoubt, left little room for political stragglers. Shortly after being elected to the Confederation Congress, Hamilton submitted a resolution announcing that "the situation of the states is in a peculiar manner critical." And the only remedy was to call a convention "to revise and amend the confederation." The delegates promptly buried the resolution in a pile of papers, never to be seen again. The most provocative feature of Hamilton's resolution was its claim that, since a national mentality did not exist, the only way to generate a population capable of "thinking Continentally" was to impose a national government on them, whether they wanted it or not.[8]

Madison was the exact opposite of Hamilton: cautious, disarmingly shy, almost invisible amid the flamboyant orators of the Virginia Dynasty. His style, in effect, was not to have one. His trademark talent was superior preparation. Though not trained as a lawyer, he thought like one, and late in 1785 began to focus his prosecutorial talents on the current practice of the states, which were passing tariffs restricting trade on one another. Impressed with the cogency of Madison's argument against the practice, in January 1786 Congress approved a convention at Annapolis to reform the rules governing interstate commerce. Madison recognized it as a small-scale effort in reforming the Articles, but perhaps a first step, "as the public mind becomes prepared for further remedies." He had no way of knowing that the Annapolis Convention would succeed beyond his wildest dreams, and do so because it failed.[9]

Only five states showed up (Virginia, New York, Pennsylvania, Delaware, and New Jersey). All the delegates could do was meet and vote to adjourn. At that dispiriting moment, Hamilton rose to the occasion in a display of almost preposterous audacity. There was a prevailing sense among the delegates, so Hamilton claimed, that the confederation was on the verge of dissolution, and reforms were necessary "to render the constitution of the Federal Government adequate to the exigencies of the union." There was therefore, or so he claimed, unanimous support for "a future Convention" with a roving mandate to address the most salient issues.* Hamilton even provided the time and place of the proposed convention: in Philadelphia, on the second Sunday in May 1787. It was as if a prizefighter, having just been knocked out by a journeyman boxer, declared his intention to challenge the heavyweight champion of the world.[10]

o o o

One obvious way to reduce the odds was to recruit America's singular figure—obvious because no one was a more outspoken

---

* When Madison learned that several delegates were on the way to Annapolis, sufficient to generate a majority, Hamilton decided to act quickly, before they arrived, lest they block his more radical agenda.

nationalist than George Washington, who had spent the entire war bemoaning the way the state legislatures had kept the Continental Army on mere life support, thereby prolonging the conflict and putting the outcome at risk. As soon as the Confederation Congress endorsed Hamilton's brazen proposal to call a constitutional convention, Madison launched the campaign to convince Washington that history was about to happen in Philadelphia and that the outcome would determine the fate of the Washington legacy:

> We can no longer doubt that the crisis is arrived at which the good people of America are to decide the solemn question, whether they will reap the fruits of that Independence and of that Union which they have cemented with so much of their blood, or whether by giving way to unmanly jealousies and prejudices, or to partial and transitory interests, they will renounce the auspicious blessings prepared for them by the Revolution, and furnish its enemies an eventual triumph.[11]

Jay had written a similar letter a few days earlier, which Washington chose to answer with a clear and uncompromising rejection. "Having happily assisted in bringing the ship into port," he explained, "and having been fairly discharged, it is not my business to embark again on a Sea of troubles." His dramatic resignation in 1783 had been widely described as the act of an American Cincinnatus. As a result, the script for this play had already been written by the gods. Cincinnatus could never come back.[12]

That sacred vow was perfectly aligned with Washington's personal sense that he was entering the last chapter of his life. As he put it to Lafayette, "I have had my day." To be told, as several friends were now telling him, that he was, once again, the indispensable man, "that those who began, carried on, and consummated the revolution, can yet rescue America from impending ruin," was flattering. But his aching bones told him otherwise. "To see this country happy whilst I am gliding down the stream of life in tranquil retirement," he explained, "was so much the wish of my soul, that nothing on this side of Elysium can be placed in competition with it."[13]

These vows of permanent retirement were surely heartfelt, but Washington had never encountered such a relentless pursuer on "this side of Elysium" as James Madison. Moreover, there was a certain irony about his resistance, because Madison was attempting to recruit him to a cause that Washington was on record as caring about more than anyone else. "No Man in the United States is, or can be more deeply impressed with the necessity of reform in the present Confederation than myself," he acknowledged to Hamilton. "In a word," he declared to anyone who would listen, "the Confederation appears to be little more than an empty sound and Congress a nugatory body."[14]

But Washington and his three courtiers were looking through different ends of the same telescope. Washington assumed that a national government could only come into existence after the American people voluntarily embraced a national identity. "We are either a United people or we are not," he explained to Madison. "If the former, let us in all matters of general concern act as a nation. If we are not, let us no longer act a force by pretending to it." In the view of Hamilton, Jay, and Madison, however, he had it backward.[15]

A national government, imposed from above, needed to come first, and over time generate a national mentality on that vast congregation of independent souls called "the people." Washington had actually glimpsed the alternative idea when he predicted that the management of the western domain would force the confederated states to cooperate as political partners. But the political agenda of his three aspiring co-conspirators envisioned a campaign to overthrow the current confederation and replace it with a government fully empowered to make domestic and foreign policy for all the states. A national mentality needed to be imposed. He was being invited to join a coup d'état.

Throughout the early spring of 1787, Washington remained resolutely opposed to ending his retirement at Mount Vernon, but his chief argument shifted. Based on conversations with several old friends from the war years, he argued that the looming convention in Philadelphia was likely to repeat the abject failure at Annapolis, and he was therefore unwilling to commit his reputation to a lost cause. Madison then went into high gear, providing updated reports on a state-by-state basis of the delegates chosen to attend the convention. His research revealed that, unlike at Annapolis, a quorum would be present in Philadelphia, that only Rhode Island would fail to show up. Moreover, most of the opponents of reform had decided to boycott the convention, thereby confining the debate to advocates of moderate and radical reform. With Washington on board, the prospect for thoroughgoing reform of the Articles was realistic, if not assured.

Madison's canvass of the state delegations altered Washington's sense of the odds. Although he remained uncertain about surrendering his cherished identity as the American Cincinnatus, as he put it, "again appearing in a public theater after a public declaration of the contrary," by late March he had decided to join the Virginia delegation in Philadelphia. (Madison had already signed him up.) But he demanded and received a commitment from Madison that "the convention would adopt no temporizing expedient, but probe the defects of the Constitution to the bottom. The goal must be radical cures, whether they are agreed to or not." This implicitly meant that Washington was agreeing to join a coup, because he was insisting that only a total replacement of the Articles justified his participation, and that meant violating the mandate from the Confederation Congress, which called for only modest reform. But in Madison's calculation, such concerns were irrelevant. With Washington aboard, the improbable had become possible.[16]

As the date of the convention in Philadelphia approached, Madison came under increasing pressure to lower his sights. Edmund Randolph—the current governor of Virginia, with long bloodlines as a member of the Tidewater aristocracy—warned Madison that all his friends believed that modest reform of the Articles was the best one could hope for. Replacing them altogether was preposterously unrealistic, the eighteenth-century equivalent of hitting the lottery. But Madison would not budge. He had promised Washington that "radical attempts, although unsuccessful, will at least justify the authors of them." And if you lost Washington, well, why bother to attend the convention?[17]

∘ ∘ ∘

As the date for the meeting in Philadelphia loomed, Madison's lawyerlike mind went into high gear as he prepared his case against the arguments he anticipated from moderates still infatuated with some semblance of the confederation framework. At first glance, his "Notes on Ancient and Modern Confederacies" seems strange, a tedious review of Greek, Italian, Dutch, and Germanic confederations over a thousand years of European history. All the stories were boringly similar, tales of temporary stability that eventually dissolved into economic and political infighting. The vast majority of confederations degenerated into separate states that went to war against one another.[18]

This predictable pattern was Madison's main point, which he made more explicitly in "Vices of the Political System of the United States," which read like a prosecuting attorney's brief against the Articles as a viable government. The litany of failures went on for thirteen pages: the states had refused to honor their tax obligations during the war and their promises to fund veterans' pensions after the war; they had refused to cooperate on internal improvements like roads and canals, and even imposed tariffs on one another;

they had signed separate treaties with various Indian tribes, essentially stealing Native American land to line the pockets of local land speculators; they had imposed their local and state interests so myopically that neither a coherent foreign policy nor a uniform system of justice was possible. The list kept going. Anyone coming to Philadelphia intending to defend the government under the Articles could expect to be buried beneath an avalanche of Madisonian invective.[19]

There is one quite obvious failure under the Articles that did not make it onto Madison's list. Nor was it mentioned, even glancingly, in the correspondence that Jay, Hamilton, and Madison shared with one another and then with Washington over the proceeding months as they planned the coup. Total silence on the slavery question was itself a loud statement that slavery was a taboo topic. If it was politically essential to have Washington on the team, it was equally essential to keep slavery off the agenda. The irony was obvious: the only way to end slavery was to create a national government empowered to make domestic policy for the states, but placing emancipation on the agenda in Philadelphia instantly destroyed any realistic prospect for creating such a government. As a result, slavery was destined to become the proverbial "Ghost at the Banquet" that defined the parameters of the possible at the convention throughout the summer of 1787.

o o o

Bad weather up and down the eastern seaboard delayed many delegates, but the obsessively prepared and prompt Madison managed to arrive in Philadelphia over a week early, on May 3. The seven-man Virginia delegation trickled in during the next two weeks, Washington on May 13, all waiting for a quorum to arrive. That left twelve days for the Virginians to caucus over food and drink at City Tavern and the African Queen. Madison seized the opportunity to lobby his Virginia colleagues, some of whom, like George Mason and Edmund Randolph, needed convincing, to assume a united front in support of a radical agenda rather than a moderate one. The selection of Washington as president of the convention was a foregone conclusion.[20]

During these preconvention sessions, the Virginians were joined by two members of the Pennsylvania delegation, Gouverneur Morris and James Wilson. Both were committed nationalists destined to play crucial roles over the ensuing months. Hamilton and Jay were not present—Hamilton because of the weather, Jay because Governor George Clinton had blocked his appointment to the New York delegation for unstated political reasons. Translation: Jay was too independent.

The fruit of their labors was the fifteen-point Virginia Plan, which was designed to set the agenda for replacing the Articles with a fully empowered federal government. The key provisions were the creation of a tripartite government modeled on the state constitutions with an executive branch, a bicameral legislature, and a judiciary; allocation of representation in both branches of the legislature by population; and an executive council that included federal judges with veto power over all state legislation. Though slavery was not explicitly mentioned, the Virginia Plan had obvious antislavery implications, chiefly in its insistence that sovereignty would be shifted from the state to the national level.[21]

For all defenders of the status quo, the Virginia Plan represented a second coup. The first coup was the calling of the Constitutional Convention itself, which they regarded as a hijacking of the ongoing debate about the Articles by an organized minority of alarmists, who had somehow recruited Washington to lend legitimacy to their dubious cause. Now the Virginia Plan represented a capture of the convention itself by imposing a national agenda as the basis for the looming debates. No one on the moderate side of the argument had come up with equivalently clear alternatives, so the Virginia Plan commanded the field by default. This tactical victory was sealed on May 30, when a majority of the delegates— only seven states were present—endorsed the resolution, proposed by Gouverneur Morris, "for a national government consisting of a supreme legislature, executive, and judiciary." The national agenda was now firmly in the saddle, and Washington comfortably in the president's chair. Madison could hardly have hoped for more.[22]

○ ○ ○

For the next fifteen weeks, from May 25 to September 17, an ever-shifting group of delegates from twelve states met in general sessions, committees, and informal gatherings in local taverns. Looked upon as a collective, the fifty-five delegates were surprisingly young—average age forty-four. They were also disproportionally well educated. Twenty-one had college degrees, and the same number had studied law. Their educational backgrounds were more conspicuous than their wealth, making them more an intellectual than an economic elite. Thirty-five had served as officers in the Continental Army, and forty-two had served in the Continental or Confederation Congress, which meant that a sizable majority of the delegates had had personal exposure to the inadequacy of the Articles during and after the war. More panoramically, as a reflection of popular opinion at the time, they were an extremely unrepresentative body, predisposed to a nationalist perspective that very few of their constituents shared.

More symbolically, the venue chosen for the convention was the East Room of the redbrick Pennsylvania State House, the same room in which the Declaration of Independence had been debated and signed. Modern tourists are often surprised at the small size of the room—with its Windsor chairs arranged in arcs facing Washington's high-backed semi-throne, the tall windows with green drapes, and small tables with green coverings—more a seminar room than an amphitheater.[23]

Opponents of the Virginia Plan were poised to argue that any significant revision of the Articles constituted a repudiation of the core values of the American Revolution. By choosing the same building, even the same room where those values were first discovered and declared, the nationalists could argue that the convention, properly understood, was a continuation rather than a rejection of "the spirit of '76," not a break with the past but an expression of its full meaning. And no less a figure than Washington himself was nodding in agreement from his high-backed wooden chair.[*]

During the second day of the convention, a procedural motion was made, without fanfare or opposition, that the one-state one-vote principle enshrined in the Articles would continue to apply at the convention. This was a deceptively consequential decision, for it meant that the small states and the slave states of the deep south, who shared a commitment to state sovereignty, could block any features of the Virginia Plan that imposed a national agenda on the states. Madison's cherished commitment to an executive veto of all state legislation was therefore dead on arrival. And the small states by themselves, which were sure to oppose proportional representation in both branches of Congress, had the votes to do it. Before the convention had barely begun, some combination of gridlock or compromise between nationalists and confederalists had become inevitable.[24]

Another procedural decision made at the start would turn out to have an abiding influence on the deliberations in Philadelphia and the way they would be regarded by posterity: the decision that

---

[*] Although the word "slavery" does not appear anywhere in the Constitution, Washington's trusted manservant Billy Lee stood beside his master's chair throughout the convention. And thirty-four of the delegates were slaveowners.

absolute secrecy must prevail, "that nothing spoken in the House be printed or otherwise published, or communicated without leave." There would be no journalists or spectators in attendance, and delegates were prohibited from discussing the debates in public or in correspondence.[25]

Moreover, thanks to the impressive detective work of Mary Sarah Bilder, we now know that Madison's *Notes, of Debates in the Federal Convention of 1787*, previously regarded as the most detailed and reliable account of the debates at the convention, are not really reliable at all; that Madison made multiple changes in *Notes* over the years that reflected his own shifting opinions on both the sovereignty question and slavery. Add to this troubling revelation the long-standing realization that the most consequential conversations about the slavery issue never made it into the official record at all, because they occurred "out of doors," in taverns, hotel rooms, and private homes. Though we obviously know what the words in the Constitution say—in fact, it is the most studied and written-about document in American history—we know very little about the covert deliberations, the arguments, concessions, and compromises, that generated and shaped those words.[26]

It does seem plausible, even probable, that the authors of the Virginia Plan and the most ardent nationalists lobbied behind the scene to keep slavery off the agenda. This was not a proslavery tactic but, rather, a realistic assessment that the slavery question must be deferred until a government empowered to make domestic policy was in place. Otherwise, the sectional split over slavery between northern and southern states would destroy the consensus necessary to reach the promised land, which was a national government that replaced the Articles. The clearest evidence of this strategy was the absence of the words "slave" and "slavery" in any of the early drafts or the final draft of the Constitution.

Although the avoidance strategy may have worked at the verbal

level, it quickly became obvious that slavery was an embedded feature in the economies of all the southern states, and that the delegates, most especially from South Carolina and Georgia, would
only join the nationalist side of the debate if they were assured that
"that species of property" was guaranteed a credible measure of
protection by the national government that emerged from Philadelphia. Without such assurance, they did not need to secede from
the union as in 1861, they needed only to block passage of the Constitution, which meant that the state-based government under the
Articles of Confederation would remain in place.

The vast majority of ordinary Americans would have been satisfied with that outcome, since the initiative to replace the Articles
had been launched by a tiny elite of nationalists, acting in open
defiance of popular opinion, with a realistic sense that they were
gambling against the odds. Historians can argue convincingly that
the founders failed to make the Constitution a document with
clear antislavery implications, and David Waldstreicher has done
just that with impressive mastery of the available evidence. The
only problem with this morally correct approach is that no document that met our modern-day standard of social justice—in effect,
any document that refused to make compromises with the slave
states of the deep south—could ever have been passed or ratified.
Which in turn meant that the United States would have remained
a confederation of sovereign states, precisely the political framework adopted by the Confederate States of America in 1861.[27]

Moreover, all historians who go back to the Constitutional
Convention with a presentistic political agenda, whether to claim
the Constitution was a proslavery or an insufficiently antislavery
document, invariably distort the multidimensional and interactive
context of the ongoing debate. Madison's much-quoted remark,
made years later, that "the states were divided into different interest, not by their difference in size, but principally from their having
or not having slaves," is partially true, but also partially false.[28]

o o o

In fact, the dominant issue at the convention throughout June and early July was a debate, which had nothing directly to do with slavery, between the large and small states over representation in both houses of Congress. Speaking for the small states, New Jersey proposed that representation must be by state rather than population. Madison and his co-conspirators in promoting the Virginia Plan initially refused to budge on this issue, since it retained the state-based structure of the Articles, and for several weeks the convention was deadlocked. A grim and somber mood began to settle in as the impasse seemed to suggest that the convention would go the way of the fiasco at Annapolis. Washington confessed he now had doubts about lending his prestige to such a problematic venture: "I almost despair of seeing a favorable issue to the proceeding of the Convention," he wrote to Hamilton, "and do therefore regret at having any urging in this business."[29]

Benjamin Franklin, also sensing that the convention was on the verge of dissolution, proposed that the delegates invite a chaplain to read a prayer. (This seems strange coming from America's most prominent deist, but it happened.) Legend has it that Hamilton rose to oppose the proposal, saying he "saw no reason to call in foreign aid." But the clever retort is probably apocryphal. If God or the gods did speak to the delegates in this critical moment, the political message was clear: appoint a committee to find a compromise solution.[30]

What came to be called the Great Compromise was a classic split-the-difference solution, making representation proportional to population in the House, and state-based in the Senate, with two representatives for each state, to be chosen by the state legislatures. The crucial vote on the committee report came on July 16. Madison and Gouverneur Morris delivered passionate pleas for the opposition that urged proportional representation in both branches of Congress, Morris somewhat melodramatically predicting civil war if the new government did not accurately represent the will of all its citizens. But the nationalists were destined to lose the debate, in part because voting in the convention followed the state-based model under the Articles they were attempting to overthrow, and in part because defeat of the compromise was widely regarded as the last act of the convention.[31]

Writing in code to Jefferson in Paris, Madison shared his deep disappointment at the outcome, which blasted his hopes for a fully empowered national government. "I hazard the opinion," he lamented, "that the plan will neither effectively answer the National project nor prevent the local mischiefs which everywhere excite disgust." The new political framework was going to be partly national and party federal, thereby leaving the all-important sovereignty question almost deliberately ambiguous. If there was an inflection point during the convention, this was it, and it had nothing directly to do with slavery.[32]

Nothing nearly so decisive occurred during the prolonged debate over the executive branch, four long sessions in June, July, and August. There were in fact two ghosts at the banquet: slavery, which was so threatening that it could not be mentioned out loud; and monarchy, which was a specter so sinister that delegates could not stop talking about it as the most dreaded ghost of all. Trying to follow the flow of the argument over executive authority during the four debates is an inherently impossible task, because there was no flow, just a series of erratic waves.[33]

Should the president be a single person or a triumvirate representing the northern, middle, and southern states? Should he serve for four, seven, twelve, or twenty years? How should he be elected, by state legislatures, by both branches of Congress, or by popular vote of all citizens? Was the office chiefly symbolic, since the title of "president" implied that his major function was to preside? On June 18, Alexander Hamilton rose to deliver a six-hour speech that dared to use the dreaded word, calling for "an elected monarch" who would serve for life. (Hamilton's best biographer described the speech as "brilliant, courageous, and completely daft.") For the remainder of Hamilton's career, the speech was used against him as evidence of his dangerously monarchical instincts. [34]

Late in their deliberations, the delegates invented that strange creature that continues to befuddle foreign observers called the Electoral College. It emerged in response to delegates favoring the popular election of the president by all qualified voters. Multiple critics objected on the grounds that popular opinion was notoriously unreliable, easily seduced by demagogues, predisposed toward conspiracy theories, an inherently inadequate expression of the larger public interest. These raw and unreliable opinions needed to be filtered through more informed and educated minds, what Madison called "filtration," chosen by the state legislators and collectively called the Electoral College.[35]

As much as or more than any other feature of the Constitution, the thought process that produced the Electoral College exposed the fact that the word "democracy" was an epithet throughout the founding era, not quite as dangerous as "monarchy," or nearly as explosive as "slavery," but nevertheless troubling for its sinister and seductive appeal to gullible majorities. Whether the United States would remain a confederation or become a nation was the great question of the moment in Philadelphia that sultry summer. But there was no question that, whatever the outcome, the government that emerged would be a republic. Not until the Age of Jackson would "democracy" earn its way into the political lexicon as an endorsement instead of an epithet.

o o o

There were in fact four sectional compromises over slavery that found their way into the Constitution, and that future abolitionists could and did characterize as a "covenant with death." Two of the compromises occurred behind closed doors, and two occurred after open debate for the public record. What is missing on all four occasions, with Gouverneur Morris the conspicuous exception, is the moral dimension of the debate. Delaware's John Dickinson recorded his personal concern that the political exchanges by both sides seemed oblivious to the larger implications of the slavery question, though he kept his reservations to himself:

> Acting before the World, what will be said of this new principle of founding a right to govern Freemen on a power derived from slaves, who are themselves incapable of governing, yet giving to others what they have not. The omitting of the WORD will be regarded as an endeavor to conceal a principle of which we are ashamed.[36]

The first debate proved the most tumultuous and occupied the delegates throughout the middle weeks of July. The issue was how to count population for representation in the House, which later affected representation in the Electoral College. The southern states wanted slaves counted as full persons, which was a complete reversal of the position they had taken during the war; at that time, the issue at stake was taxation, not representation, and they argued that slaves were property, not persons, and therefore should not be counted. The compromise was the three-fifths clause, an invention by a younger Madison during an earlier debate in the Confederation Congress. It was intended not as a moral statement about the lesser human value of slaves, but as a political compromise about how to count them as part persons, part property, for deciding representation in the House.

The debate is extremely hard to follow, akin to watching a soccer match played with two balls and no referees, in part because the key players kept changing sides, and neither side was satisfied by the split-the-difference outcome. The successful resolution was made by Edmund Randolph of Virginia, affirming that representation in the House would be predicated on "a periodic census based on the numbers of whites and three-fifths of the blacks." The political advantage the three-fifths clause gave to southern states in presidential elections was the main reason that Jefferson was referred to as "the Negro president" after his narrow victory in the election of 1800.[37]

o o o

The second compromise with slavery occurred in the immediate wake of the three-fifths compromise. It occurred not in Philadelphia but in New York, where multiple delegates from the southern states traveled, both to provide a quorum in the moribund Confederation Congress and to cast a vote in favor of the Northwest Ordinance. All the southern delegates voted for Article VI of that ordinance, which stipulated, "There shall be neither slavery nor involuntary servitude in the said territory. . . ." The unanimous vote by representatives of proslavery states to prohibit the expansion of slavery into the Northwest Territory confounded all observers at the time, and has mystified historians ever since.

Several explanations have been offered, but the most probable, though unprovable, explanation is that a silent agreement between northern and southern delegates had been reached at the convention in Philadelphia, less a "grand bargain" than a "mutual understanding" that the southern states would endorse the prohibition of slavery in the Northwest Territories if the northern states complied by refusing to oppose its extension in the Southwest Territories. That, in any event, is what happened during the following decades, when the territories of Kentucky, Tennessee, and Alabama entered the union.

Nothing was written into the Constitution formalizing any of those sectional compromises. But it is quite possible, indeed probable, that we are witnessing an unspoken agreement that the expansion of the infant American republic across the continent toward the Mississippi would occur on the shared presumption that the northwest would project the antislavery values of the northern states, and the southwest would embody the proslavery values of the southern states.[38]

o o o

The third compromise with slavery occurred late in the convention, and took the form of a bargain between the New England states and the states of the deep south on the question of the slave trade. Until then, with the exception of the heated debate over a three-fifths clause, Madison and his co-conspirators had done an admirable job of keeping slavery off the agenda. In August, however, the prospect of resuming the slave trade generated a gush of eloquence from the long-suppressed antislavery convictions of several delegates.

Gouverneur Morris, the towering peg-legged raconteur with a reputation as a wit (and a way with other men's wives), ignited the explosion with the first frontal assault on the institution of slavery itself. Not content to condemn slavery as "a moral travesty," Morris compared the burgeoning economies of the northern states with "the misery and poverty which overspread the barren wastes of Virginia and the other states having slaves." As far as the slave trade was concerned, Morris found it impossible to understand "the inhabitant of Georgia and South Carolina who goes to the coast of Africa, and in defiance of the most sacred laws of humanity, tears away his fellow creatures from their dearest connections and damns them to the most cruel bondage." His two-hour speech was greeted with dead silence. Morris had torn the lid off Pandora's box.[39]

Eventually, Luther Martin of Maryland and George Mason of

Virginia rose to endorse Morris's condemnation of the slave trade. Martin was already famous for his bombastic style, usually fueled by multiple sips of whiskey, but he mustered up uncharacteristic cogency when he concluded that the slave trade was "inconsistent with values of the revolution and [it was] dishonorable to the American character to have such a feature in the Constitution." Mason was the temperamental opposite of Martin, renowned as Virginia's leading constitutional thinker, somehow capable of almost preternatural serenity on his feet. On the slave trade, Mason was characteristically succinct: "I hold it essential in every point of view that the general government should have the power to prevent the increase of slavery."[40]

In response to such passionate and public criticisms, South Carolina reacted with calm defiance. John Rutledge, the most prominent politician in the state, brushed aside all moral arguments against slavery or the slave trade. "Religion and humanity had nothing to do with the question," he boldly declared. "Interest alone is the governing principle with nations." Rutledge then issued the ultimate challenge. The only question was "whether the Southern states shall or shall not be parties to the Union." Charles Pinckney, his South Carolina colleague, echoed the same threat: "South Carolina can never receive the plan if it prohibits the slave trade." No northern state had ever uttered the same ultimate threat on the slavery or slave-trade issue, or played the same game of brinkmanship. Once again, as with the earlier debate over representation in the House, the convention was deadlocked. And, once again, the obvious answer was to send the matter to a committee.[41]

After much backing and forthing, the committee proposed a sectional compromise: The New England states would agree to support the extension of the slave trade until 1800, later lengthened to 1808. In return, South Carolina and Georgia would agree to accept a change whereby all legislation regulating imports and exports would require only a simple majority rather than a two-thirds supermajority, which significantly reduced the ability of the states in the deep south to block tariffs on incoming slaves and outgoing rice and indigo. The bargain endorsed the resumption of the slave trade, but only temporarily, and during subsequent debates in the ratifying conventions in several northern states, 1808 loomed large as the agreed-upon date when the larger question of slavery itself could be safely placed on the national agenda. In their opinion, the compromise with evil had a limited lifespan.[42]

On the other hand, the temporary extension of the slave trade had enormous long-term consequences. Between 1788 and 1808 more than two hundred thousand African slaves were imported to the United States. Add those numbers to the five hundred thousand slaves already in place, and more accruing exponentially every decade, and the result was a demographic explosion that only strengthened the political prowess of the slave south. Put differently, if there had ever been a chance to put slavery on the road to extinction south of the Potomac, the convention had just missed it.

ọ ọ ọ

The fourth and final compromise, the fugitive slave clause, occurred near the very end of the convention. (If the historian would be granted a one-time opportunity at second guessing, this would be it.)* On August 29, Pierce Butler of South Carolina made the following proposal:

> If any person bound to serve or labor in any of the U. States shall not be discharged from such service or from which they escape, they shall be delivered to the person justly claiming their service or labor.[43]

* The South Carolina delegation was surprised to get this concession. And it was highly unlikely that they would have walked if the northern states had refused to support it.

The proposal passed unanimously, without debate. It not only explicitly endorsed slavery, but also required those states where slavery had been abolished to become explicitly complicitous in holding slaves in bondage. More than any other provision in the Constitution, it required all the states to publicly acknowledge the abiding existence of slavery. One is almost obliged to ask, "What were they thinking?"

Three overlapping answers come to mind: first, the delegates were all tired, several had already escaped the Philadelphia heat, a bare quorum remained, and they all wanted to go home; second, the South Carolina and Georgia delegations had recently discovered the political prowess of their threat to bolt the convention if not appeased on the slave-trade issue, and were therefore poised to enhance the momentum of that advantage; third, the northern states cared more about preserving the union than they cared about ending slavery, while the priorities of the states in the deep south were precisely the opposite.

o o o

There was another, more positive way to put it, and that task was taken up by Benjamin Franklin in the last speech delivered at the Convention. At eighty-one, Franklin was the oldest man in the room, the grandfather among the fathers. He was also afflicted with kidney stones and gout, but was one of the few delegates, along with Madison, to attend almost every session; he was carried on an elaborate sedan by four husky prisoners from the local jail. Most of his comments at the convention were read for him by James Wilson, his Pennsylvania colleague, and were often off point or politically eccentric, like his proposal for a single-house legislature in the mode of the Pennsylvania Constitution. But his international reputation as second only to Washington in stature meant that the other delegates humored his suggestions and never questioned his judgment. There was an unspoken consensus that he was not only the oldest but the wisest man in the room.

Franklin was also acting president of the Pennsylvania Abolitionist Society and, knowing full well that he was much closer to the end than the beginning, had decided to make abolition the central focus of his last chapter. In early June, just after the convention was getting started, he had received a lengthy proposal from the Abolitionist Society, most of it a passionate denunciation of the slave trade, but with one section declaring that slavery was a blatant contradiction of the core values of the American Revolution. At this early stage of the convention, the prominent nationalists were rallying behind the Virginia Plan, as well as behind the clear conviction that slavery must be kept off the political agenda. Several delegates urged Franklin to put the proposal from the Abolitionist Society in his pocket, and Franklin reluctantly followed that advice for the remainder of the convention. He was also conspicuously silent when the forbidden topic burst out into the open in mid- and late August. His eloquent speech at the end of the convention, though it never mentions slavery, should be read in the context of that prolonged silence.

I confess that I do not entirely approve this Constitution at present, but Sir, I am not sure I shall never approve it. For having lived long, I have experienced many instances of being obliged, by better Information or fuller Considerations, to change opinion on important Subjects, Which I once thought Right, but found to be otherwise. It is therefore that the older I grow, the more apt I am to doubt my own judgment, and to pay more respect to the Judgment of others.

In these Sentiments, Sir, I agree with this Constitution, with all its Faults, if they are such, because I think a General Government necessary for us. I doubt too whether any other Convention we can obtain may be able to make a better Constitution.

It therefore astonished me, Sir, to find this System approaching so near to Perfection as it does; and I think it will astonish our Enemies, who are waiting with confidence to hear that our Councils are Confounded, like those of the Builders of Babel, and that our States are on the point of Separation, only to meet, hereafter, for the Purpose of cutting one another's throats. Thus I consent, Sir, to this Constitution, because I expect no better, and I am not sure it is not the best.[44]

Franklin's central point was that everyone needed to adjust their expectations, that neither political perfection nor moral purity was ever in the cards at the Constitutional Convention. For, once a tiny slate of ardent nationalists had quite craftily hijacked the political conversation, captured George Washington's endorsement, and manipulated the agenda in Philadelphia, compromise on the most controversial issues, slavery most of all, was both unavoidable and inevitable. Most elementally, any fully national government needed to include the southern states, who could be expected to insist on some measure of protection for their enslaved workforce.

Therefore, the presumption that slavery could be kept off the agenda had always been a delusion. When Franklin acknowledged that he had "not entirely approved this Constitution," he was probably referring to the four compromises on slavery required to assure the southern votes for passage of the Constitution. One could quibble about this compromise or that, but the moral argument against any compromise at all was just as delusional as the belief that the slavery issue could be finessed. It might have made sense at a Quaker meeting, but the Constitutional Convention was not a gathering designed to separate the saints from the sinners. It was more like a marriage ceremony in which the northern and southern states, despite their differences, decided they could live together in peace.

Several years later, Gouverneur Morris, the most outspoken opponent of slavery at the convention, echoed Franklin's realistic advice in just such terms. "In adopting a republican form of government," Morris joked, "I not only took it as a man does a wife, for better or for worse, but what few men do with their wives, I took it knowing all the bad qualities." The sectional marriage was fated to last for seventy-four years, until 1861, when it became clear that the two sections had never agreed about what "better or worse" meant. Indeed, well over two centuries later, they still don't agree on the racial implications of The Cause.[45]

Chapter 6

The Epilogue

o o o

Whatever veneration might be entertained for the body of
men who formed our constitution, the sense of that body
could never be regarded as an oracular guide. As the instru-
ment came from them, it was nothing more but a dead letter, until life and validity were breathed into it by the several
state conventions.

—JAMES MADISON in Congress, April 6, 1796

THE DEBATES THROUGHOUT the summer of 1787 in Philadelphia had been conducted in total secrecy, without press
coverage or any attempt to keep the public informed about
the deliberations. So, when the final draft of the Constitution was
released to the world in September, it came as a complete surprise.
Who knew that a few men would propose, not a mere revision, but
a complete overhaul of the current arrangement under the Articles?

Between the early fall of 1787 and midsummer 1788, 1,646 delegates from twelve states—Rhode Island continued its boycott—
met in ratifying conventions. The arguments that ensued in the
conventions as well as town meetings and family parlors from
Maine to Georgia were spirited affairs. And unlike the debates at
the Constitutional Convention, these debates were fully recorded

and widely covered by the press, generating a sprawling historical account that almost defies succinct summary. For every state was different, and within every state there were sectional splits with competing priorities of their own.

There was, however, an overall pattern: namely, every state viewed the proposed Constitution through the lens of its own state and local interests. As a result, what came to be called the Great Debate was actually a Great Cacophony. No such thing as a national ethos existed out there where ordinary Americans lived their blissful ordinary lives. They thought of themselves not as Americans but, rather, as Pennsylvanians, Virginians, or Georgians. The ratification debate, then, was a hydra-headed monster that exposed the counterintuitive fact that Alexander Hamilton had foreseen much earlier: no such thing as American nationhood existed, so it had to be created by establishing a national government that gradually forced itself on an otherwise provincial population.[1]

There was, to be sure, a deep sectional divide between northern and southern states over the issue of slavery, which we will shortly examine. But there was a deeper divide between nationalists and confederationists, the later preferring a modest reform of the Articles that left the sovereignty of states intact. They were an overwhelming majority, in part because they spoke for the local mentality of most citizens, in part because they could claim that any powerful central government represented a second coming of Parliament, which The Cause had purportedly banished forever. At first blush, then, the confederationists, who called themselves Anti-Federalists, appeared to enjoy a decisive advantage. But, as it turned out, they did not.[*] The following chart provides a succinct

---

[*] In the debate between Federalists and Anti-Federalists, the former enjoyed the advantage of superior leadership from Hamilton, Madison, and Jay, the three co-conspirators who made the convention happen, and who then came together again to produce *The Federalist Papers,* which became an American classic.

summary, in chronological order, of the ratification process in all thirteen states.

STATE	DATE	YAY / NAY
Delaware	December 7, 1787	30–0
Pennsylvania	December 12, 1787	46–23
New Jersey	December 18, 1787	38–0
Georgia	December 31, 1787	26–0
Connecticut	January 8, 1788	128–40
Massachusetts	February 6, 1788	187–168 *(with amendments)*
Maryland	April 26, 1788	63–11
South Carolina	May 26, 1788	149–73
New Hampshire	June 21, 1788	57–47 *(with amendments)*
Virginia	June 29, 1788	89–79 *(with amendments)*
New York	July 26, 1788	30–27 *(with amendments)*
North Carolina	November 21, 1789	194–77 *(with amendments)*
Rhode Island	May 29, 1790	34–32 *(with amendments)*

At first glance, the chart suggests that ratification of the Constitution enjoyed widespread popular support. Majorities in several states were overwhelming, and, in the end, not a single state, not even Rhode Island, refused to ratify. On the face of it, the Great Debate produced a resounding vote for American nationhood.[2]

A closer look, however, tends to undermine that comfortable conclusion. During the final days of the Constitutional Convention, the delegates passed a resolution requiring the states to appoint special ratifying conventions rather than delegate the decision to the state legislatures. According to John Marshall, an ardent nationalist and future chief justice of the Supreme Court, a sizable majority of Virginians opposed ratification, "but they have chosen their most trusted local leaders as delegates, who by a small margin support it." The same pattern that Marshall witnessed in Virginia occurred in most of the states, making the vote on ratification less a popular referendum than a decision by the most experienced and prominent figures in each state, often the same delegates who had served in the Constitutional Convention.[3]

Moreover, the delegates in Philadelphia had decided that nine states would constitute a sufficient consensus. There was a hidden as well as an obvious advantage to the nine-vote requirement, and Madison, ever the political operative, was the first to recognize it. "It is generally believed that the nine states will embrace the plan," he predicted, "consequently that the tardy remainder must be reduced to the dilemma of either shifting for themselves or coming in without any credit for it." The chronological sequence of the ratifying conventions only enhanced this momentum factor. Because Virginia and New York—two of the largest states, where opposition was most formidable—came late to the schedule, pressure to ratify would build on them once nine states had ratified, or once that outcome seemed likely.[4]

Finally, early in the ratification process several state conventions indicated that they wished to ratify, as the chart shows, "with amendments." If they had been allowed to do so, the likely outcome would have been multiple versions of the Constitution, simultaneously an accurate reflection of political opinion throughout the land and a fatal blow to the entire ratification enterprise. Madison took the lead—how he managed this feat is unclear—by insisting that all proposed amendments were only recommendations to be considered later. The vote on ratification could not be conditional, but must fit into one of two categories: aye or nay. Much like the referendum on independence in 1776, there was no middle course. It is quite likely that a majority of the citizenry would have preferred a revision of the Articles, but that option was not available.

Madison was in his nose-counting mode throughout the Great Debate, and early on he, albeit reluctantly, came to the realization that if he had gotten what he wanted in Philadelphia—namely, a strong executive branch and a Congress fully empowered to make foreign and domestic policy—his preferred Constitution would never have been ratified. In a long letter to Jefferson in October 1787, he described the hybrid character of the document that had emerged from the Constitutional Convention as a two-headed creature that was part confederation and part nation. The delegates, he observed, had "managed to draw a line of demarcation which would give the General Government every power required for general purposes, and leave to the states every power which might be most beneficial to them."[5]

Left unsaid was that no one knew where that line existed, or what "general purposes" meant. Madison realized that his push for an unambiguous resolution of the sovereignty question at the convention had been misguided, that there was no consensus in either the convention or the country on that core issue; so what they had created was a political framework that deliberately blurred the issue. They had, willy-nilly, out of necessity rather than choice, discovered the beauty of ambiguity.* The Constitution was designed not to resolve arguments but to make argument itself the answer by providing a political arena where the debate over the most contested issues could continue in a deliberative fashion. Among the contested issues, the most contested was slavery.

---

* The ambiguity was assisted by the dual meaning of "federalism" and "federal." As an adjective in, for example, "federal government," it meant the central source of political authority. As a noun, "federalism" meant shared sovereignty between the central government and the states.

o o o

The problem that historians face in exploring and explaining the debate at the Constitutional Convention is amplified by the limited and unreliable state of the evidence. The dilemma posed by the ratification debate is exactly the opposite. It is akin to sailing from the Chesapeake Bay into the Atlantic Ocean: the challenge is not to drown under the waves of evidence.

A second look at our chart can provide a measure of guidance that helps us recover the underlying reasons for the outcome. The vote in three of the largest states—Massachusetts, Virginia, and New York—was extremely close. A clear majority actually opposed ratification in New York, North Carolina, and Rhode Island, which grudgingly came in late in the game, after the nine-vote quota had been reached. The insistence on amendments in six of the states reflected a deep dissatisfaction with the all-or-nothing terms of the debate. A shift of six votes in Virginia would probably have produced a shock wave that would have left four states—Virginia, New York, North Carolina, and Rhode Island—out of the union. And even though nine states had ratified, it is difficult to imagine an American nation surviving in such a geographically splintered condition. The political elite in Virginia tended to harbor an inflated sense of their own significance, but in the debate over ratification they were right. Virginia was the all-important state.[6]

It therefore makes historical sense to focus, at least initially, on the debate in Richmond during the early summer of 1788. This also makes dramatic sense, since the debate featured a confrontation between two political giants of the age, Patrick Henry and James Madison. (To call Madison, at five foot two, a giant is, on the face of it, a misnomer, but he compensated mentally for what he lacked physically. As one commentator put it, "Never have I seen so much mind in so little matter.") Madison had been on the receiving end of Henry's eloquence on several occasions, so he knew what he was up against. Henry on his feet was a force of nature, part preacher in the pulpit, part actor on the stage, who spoke without notes, often wandering off point, but always casting a spell. In response to Madison's request for advice, Jefferson acknowledged that there was no way to deal with Henry "except to ardently pray for his imminent death."[7]

Henry began by arguing that the proposed Constitution was an illegitimate document, since the delegates in Philadelphia had violated their mandate by replacing the Articles rather than merely revising them. But the core of his argument was the claim that the first three words of the Constitution were a fictional delusion. "The question turns, sir, on that poor little thing, the expression 'We, the people' instead of 'the States of America.'" For there was no such thing as "the American people," only Virginians, Pennsylvanians, New Englanders, or South Carolinians. As a result, the delegates in Philadelphia had created a government that purported to represent a political body that did not exist. The watchword of Henry's critique was "consolidation," a term loaded with ideological implications. "You make the citizens of this country, the subjects of one consolidated empire in America," Henry warned—in effect, a domestic version of Parliament that Americans had spent so much blood and treasure to escape. When Henry spoke of "my country," he meant Virginia.[8]

Nowhere did Henry mention slavery, though his state-based vision implicitly assumed that Virginia and all the southern states could and should make their own decisions about both the slave trade and slavery itself. The most explicit version of a proslavery argument came from George Mason, an apparently strange posture for someone who had on several occasions during the Philadelphia convention delivered speeches denouncing slavery in a moralistic tone usually heard at Quaker meetings. Once back in the Old Dominion, however, Mason recovered his Virginia voice.

In a speech on June 17, 1788, he clarified his reason for not signing the Constitution, which was partly because it did not contain a bill of rights, but mostly because, as he succinctly put it, "they have done what they ought not to have done"—that is, extended the slave trade for twenty years—"and left undone what they ought to have done": that is "secured for us the property in slaves we already have."[9]

Madison rose to contest Mason's reasoning, claiming that he, too, regretted the extension of the slave trade, but reminding Mason that there were profound political reasons for embracing the compromise. "The Southern States would not have entered into the Union of America without the temporary permission of that trade," he declared, "and if they were excluded from the Union the consequences might be dreadful to them and to us." Neither Mason nor Madison mentioned that Virginia's motives for opposing the slave trade were not moral but economic. If deprived of imported slaves, the Carolinas and Georgia would become a market for Virginia's excess slaves. In effect, slaves would replace tobacco as Virginia's major cash crop.[10]

Although the close vote in Virginia was in part a function of Henry's eloquence, and in part a reluctance to surrender its sovereignty to any federal government, the decisive votes for ratification came from several western counties, to include the looming state of Kentucky, where delegates cared most about retaining navigation rights on the Mississippi. Though not irrelevant, slavery took a back seat to local and regional priorities. In Virginia, as in most of the states, the ratification process defied any single-minded analysis.

o o o

That said, if we move to a higher elevation, the most controversial compromise reached in Philadelphia by far was the resumption of the slave trade. Especially in the New England states, where ministers played a major role in the pamphlet and newspaper exchanges, the continuation of the slave trade, if not a covenant with death, was an outright surrender to sin. "How does it appear in the sight-of-heaven," wrote Reverend Samuel Hopkins of Newport, "that these States, who have been fighting for liberty, cannot agree in any political constitution unless it indulge and authorize them to enslave their fellow men."[11]

Moreover, instead of taking a small step toward ending slavery, Americans were now being asked to take a large step toward sustaining it, which Hopkins feared would eventually become a path toward civil war. The debates in Massachusetts also featured voices of opposition to the three-fifths clause and the fugitive-slave provision, but press coverage throughout New England was dominated by the decision to resume the slave trade for the next twenty years. Even delegates who voted "aye" often expressed regret at swallowing a sin.[12]

Meanwhile, down in Philadelphia, James Wilson was reading the tea leaves quite differently. Wilson, a Scotsman educated at the University of Saint Andrews, had spoken against slavery on several occasions during the convention, but was also kept busy delivering speeches for the ailing Benjamin Franklin. On December 3, Wilson rose to defend the decision to extend the slave trade. "If there was no other lovely future in the Constitution but this one," he proclaimed, "it would diffuse a beauty over its whole countenance." Why so? Because, after the lapse of a few years, "Congress will have power to exterminate slavery within our borders." Although the Constitution did not say so explicitly, Wilson claimed there was an implicit understanding, at least within the Pennsylvania delegation, that delaying the end of the slave trade for twenty years would allow the infant republic to outgrow its infancy, its most vulnerable phase, and then proceed to address what he called "the great contradiction" without fear of disunion. Moreover, during this extended deferral, "the new states which are to be formed will be under the control of congress, and slaves will never be introduced among them." As Wilson saw it, all the other compromises with slavery were historically irrelevant, since in the space of one generation slavery would be on the road to extinction.[13]

Anyone with a deep southern accent who heard Wilson's speech might well have experienced a nervous breakdown. Down in South Carolina, for example, Charles Cotesworth Pinckney, a much-decorated general during the war, was holding forth in ways that suggested that he and Wilson had attended different conventions.

"By this settlement," Pinckney declared, "we have secured an unlimited supply of negroes for twenty years; nor is it declared that the importation shall be then stopped; it may be continued; I believe it will. We have a security that the general government can never emancipate them, for no such authority is granted, and it is admitted by all hands that all rights not expressed were reserved by the several states. We have obtained a right to recover our slaves in whatever part of America they take refuge, which is a right we had not before. In short, we have made the best terms for the security of this species of property as it was in our power to make. We would have made better if we could, but on the whole, I do not think them bad."[14]

When asked to justify his confidence about the continuation of the slave trade after 1808, Pinckney dodged the question by launching a soliloquy on South Carolina's dependence on slave labor. "While there remained one acre of swamp land uncleared in South Carolina," he declared, "I will raise my voice against restricting the importation of negroes," and argued that "the swamp situation of our country obliges us to cultivate our lands with negroes, that without them S. Carolina would soon be a desert waste." When pressed, he explained that Whites never would or could do the labor of Blacks.[15]

The following day, Pinckney rose to deliver a postscript to his defense of the South Carolina delegation's performance in Philadelphia, providing a confidential report on its behind-the-scenes maneuvering. "Another reason weighed heavily with the members of this state against the insertion of a bill of rights," he revealed, "since such bills generally began by declaring that all men are by nature born free, and we should make that declaration with very bad grace, when a large part of our property consists in men who are actually born slaves."[16]

There was, in effect, a fundamental disagreement over what had happened in Philadelphia, which exposed different understandings of the decision to extend the slave trade and different expectations about the fate of slavery itself. The more mainstream view in most northern states and in pockets of Virginia was that there was an agreement to defer the whole slavery question until 1808, when the slave trade was likely to end. In the states of the deep south, the consensus was that they had been assured that, even if the slave trade ended after twenty years, the newly installed federal government had no authority to impose any restrictions on their invaluable enslaved laborers. The northern states, whether they knew it or not, had agreed to live with a contradiction forever.

o o o

From the Quaker perspective, forever meant two years. Shortly after the Constitution was ratified, on February 11, 1790, two Quaker delegations, one from New York and the other from Philadelphia, presented petitions to the House calling for the federal government to put an immediate end to the African slave trade, arguing that it was a blatant violation of the values declared to the world in the Declaration of Independence. Representative James Jackson from Georgia was immediately on his feet, rejecting the petition, shaking his fist at the Quakers in the gallery, denouncing them as infamous innocents incessantly disposed to drip their precious purity like holy water over everyone else's sins. They were also highly questionable patriots, he claimed, having sat out the recent war against British tyranny in deference to their cherished consciences. Jackson had to be restrained from further outbursts by a colleague from South Carolina, William Loughton Smith.[17]

Smith urged Jackson to calm down. True enough, the problematic patriotism of the Quaker petitioners was reprehensible, but their petition lacked standing. The recently ratified Constitution explicitly prohibited Congress from passing any law that abolished or restricted the slave trade until 1808. Several current members of Congress had served as delegates to the Constitutional Convention, and they could all testify that the document would never have been approved in Philadelphia, much less ratified by several southern states, without that provision. The Quaker petitioners, therefore, were asking for something that had been declared unavailable.[18]

Jackson, however, was not willing to be consoled. He detected even more sinister motives behind the benign smiles of the misnamed Society of Friends. "I apprehend, if through the interference of the general government the slave trade should be abolished," he observed, "it would evince to the people a general disposition toward a total emancipation." In short, the Quaker petition was really a stalking horse for a more radical scheme to end the institution of slavery itself.[19]

Madison, now serving as a Virginia representative in the House, rose to assure his colleague from Georgia that the Quaker petition would be forwarded to a committee "as a matter of course," where it would die a silent death, and "no notice would be taken of it out of doors." But Jackson's overwrought opposition, much like airbursts in a night battle, actually called attention to the issues the Quakers wished to raise. His intemperate behavior was playing into their hands. Jackson needed to restrain himself, for, as Madison assured him, "such things are not contemplated by any gentlemen in the congress."[20]

The next day, however, Jackson's fearful prophecies seemed to be coming true. On that day, another petition arrived in the House, this one from the Pennsylvania Abolition Society, urging the Congress to "take such measures in their wisdom, as the powers authorized to you will allow, for promoting the abolition of slavery, and discouraging every species of traffic in slaves." Moreover, the petition challenged the claim that the Constitution prohibited any legislation by the federal government for ending the slave trade until 1808, arguing that the "general welfare" clause of the Constitution empowered the Congress to take whatever action it deemed "necessary and proper" to eliminate "the traffic in human beings" and to countenance "the Restoration of Liberty for all Negroes." Finally, to top it off and heighten its dramatic appeal, the petition arrived under the signature of Benjamin Franklin, whose patriotic credentials and international reputation were beyond dispute. Indeed, if there were an American pantheon, only Washington had a more secure place in it than Franklin.[21]

Franklin's endorsement of the petition effectively assured that the preferred Madisonian strategy—banish the petition to the congressional version of oblivion—was not going to work. The House set aside all its regular business and put itself into committee-of-the-whole format to permit unencumbered debate for the next six hours. Things were said that had only been uttered behind the scenes at the Constitutional Convention.

The debate began when Thomas Scott of Pennsylvania acknowledged that the Constitution imposed restrictions on Congress's power to end the slave trade but said nothing whatsoever about abolishing slavery itself. "If I was one of the judges of the United States," Scott observed, "I do not know how far I would go if these people were to come before me and claim their emancipation, but I am sure I would go as far as I could." Whereupon Jackson countered by claiming that any judge rendering such an opinion in Georgia "would be of short duration."[22]

Jackson then launched into a sermon on God's will, which he described as patently proslavery, based on several passages in the Bible, which he read out loud while glaring at the Quakers in the balcony. William Loughton Smith preferred to leave the interpretation of God's will to others, but he seconded the opinion of his Georgia colleague that Georgia's entire economy depended on slave labor, insisting, "No white man would perform the tasks required to drain the swamps and clear the land, so without slaves it must be depopulated."[23]

The chief text for Smith was not the Bible but the Constitution. In addition to the explicit provision that rendered the slave trade off limits for twenty years, there was also an implicit but broadly shared understanding that the newly created federal government could do nothing to interfere with the existence of slavery in the southern states; and all such states had ratified the Constitution with that understanding as a necessary condition. "Upon that reason they acceded to the Constitution," Smith declared, and "unless that part was granted, they would never have come into the union."[24]

In response, John Laurance of New York wondered how any Christian could read the Sermon on the Mount and conclude it was compatible with slavery. Laurance acknowledged that certain provisions of the Constitution recognized the existence of slavery, but the larger understanding, as he saw it, was that slavery was an anomaly in the American republic, a condition that could be tolerated in the short run precisely because there was a clear consensus that it would be ended in the long run. Scott of Pennsylvania echoed those sentiments, adding that the defining text was not the Constitution but the Declaration of Independence. Scott also found it intriguing that both sides of the debate seemed to take refuge not in what the Constitution said but, rather, in what they thought it implied.[25]

The vote to refer Franklin's petition to a committee was surprisingly one-sided, forty-three to eleven. (Seven of the eleven negative votes came from South Carolina and Georgia.) Madison's earlier prediction that the petition would die in the committee was no longer relevant. All the northern states wanted the debate to continue, believing they had the southern states on the defensive and no less than Benjamin Franklin on their side.

o o o

While the committee was deliberating, the South Carolina and Georgia delegations resumed their attack on the Quaker petitions. William Loughton Smith pointed up to the Quakers who stacked the galleries, as Smith put it, "like evil spirits hovering over our heads." James Jackson made menacing faces at the Quakers in the gallery, called them "outright lunatics," and "shaking Quakers with throbbing consciences." There was important business before the Congress, they both observed, chiefly Alexander Hamilton's controversial financial plan, and the equally controversial decisions about where to locate the new capital city, both of which were being interrupted by a cluster of "dazed dreamers" who seemed intent on sinking the American ship of state on its maiden voyage.[26]

Then Jackson referred his colleagues to the opinion of "Mr. Jefferson, our secretary of state," and began reading from Jefferson's *Notes on the State of Virginia*, claiming that he could quote from the book from memory. The crucial issue it addressed now needed to be out on the table for both his northern and his southern colleagues: "What is to be done with the slaves when freed?"

Up until now, the central argument for slavery from the South Carolina and Georgia delegations had been chiefly economic, essentially that, without enslaved workers, their rice plantations would become worthless swamps. Now Jackson was shifting the argument from rice to race, quoting Jefferson that the two races could not live together on equal terms because of "deep rooted prejudices entertained by the whites, ten thousand recollections by the blacks of injuries they have sustained, new provocations, and the real distinctions that nature had made." Perhaps a few Whites in the north did not agree with Jefferson's sentiments, Jackson acknowledged. Perhaps the Quaker petitioners approved of racial mixing and looked forward to "giving their daughters to negro sons, and receiving the negro daughter for their sons." But despite the relatively small size of the black population in the northern states, the pattern of racial segregation there suggested that most Whites shared Jefferson's belief that "incorporation" was unlikely. In the southern states, where the numbers of Blacks was so much larger, it was unthinkable.[27]

Those advocating emancipation, then, needed to confront the intractable dilemma posed by the sheer size of the African population that, once freed, must be removed to some other location. Where was anyone's guess: Sierra Leone? The Caribbean? The American west? Jackson identified problems with all the options, and a larger problem with the astronomical costs of compensating the owners and essentially reversing a diaspora that had deposited enslaved Africans on the North American continent for well over a century. If anyone had a responsible solution to the problem, Jackson claimed to be receptive. But until such a solution materialized, all talk of emancipation must cease.

The following day, March 17, William Loughton Smith held the floor for over two hours without interruption and repeated most of Jackson's arguments. Whereas Jackson tended toward a more volatile, pulpit-thumping style reminiscent of an itinerant Presbyterian minister in the revivalistic mode, Smith preferred the more measured cadences of a South Carolina aristocrat steeped in the Ciceronian formalities. He also congratulated his Georgia colleague for exposing the racial arguments that had been bandied about behind closed doors at the Constitutional Convention, but were regarded as too inflammatory to mention in public.

Arguments based on his conversation with his constituents in South Carolina immediately surfaced once the prospect of emancipation reared its ugly head. The racial implications were unspeakably horrific. "If the blacks did not intermarry with the whites," Smith concluded, "they would remain black until the end of time; for it was not contended that liberating them would whitewash them; if they did intermarry with the whites, then the white race would become extinct, and the American people would all be of the mulatto breed. In whatever light therefore, the subject is viewed, the folly of emancipation is manifest." Smith thereby gave a new dimension to the slavery debate by attempting to transform the sectional debate between north and south into a national alliance of Whites against Blacks.[28]

o o o

No one from the northern states rose to challenge the proslavery arguments of Jackson and Smith. But down in Philadelphia, one person who was reading reports of the debate in Congress stepped forward to answer the challenge. Benjamin Franklin was both old and ill in March 1790. Unquestionably the oldest, probably the wisest member of the revolutionary generation, Franklin had been a fixture on the American scene for so long and had outlived so many of his contemporaries—the grandfather among the fathers—that reports of his imminent departure lacked credibility. He was an American immortal. The greatest American scientist, the most deft diplomat, the most accomplished prose stylist, the sharpest wit, Franklin defied all the categories by inhabiting them all with such distinction and nonchalant grace.

Seemingly eternal, ubiquitous, protean, and endlessly quotable, Franklin also had a personal reason for entering the debate. The petition from the Pennsylvania Abolitionist Society that had launched the debate had come forward under his signature. And it was a somewhat abbreviated version of the very petition he had been asked to introduce at the Constitutional Convention, but had chosen not to do based on advice from several delegates who warned that it risked a walkout by the South Carolina and Georgia delegations, which would have put the entire constitutional project in jeopardy. Now, knowing full well that he was entering his last chapter, he decided to finish the business left undone at the convention.[29]

Under the pseudonym "Historicus," Franklin published a parody of the speech delivered by James Jackson of Georgia. He claimed to have noticed an eerie similarity between Jackson's speech on behalf of slavery and one delivered a century earlier by an Algerian pirate named Sidi Mehmet Ibrahim. Surely the similarities were coincidential, Franklin explained, since Jackson was obviously an honorable man and thus incapable of plagiarism. But the arguments and language were strikingly similar, except that Jackson used Christianity to justify the enslavement of Africans, whereas the Algerians used Islam to justify the enslavement of Christians.

"The Doctrine that plundering and enslaving of Christians is unjust is at the best highly problematic," the Algerian had allegedly written, and, when presented with a petition to cease capturing Europeans, had argued to the Divan of Algiers that, since "it was in the interest of the State to continue the practice," therefore they should "let the petition be rejected without wandering into dubiously moralistic clouds." All the same practical objections to ending slavery were also raised: "But who is to indemnify their Masters for the loss? Is our Treasury sufficient? For if we set them free, what is to be done with them? Our people will not pollute themselves by intermarrying with them." The Algerian also argued that the enslaved Christians "were better off with us as slaves, rather than remain in Europe where they would only cut each other's throats in religious wars."[30]

Franklin's pointed parody was reprinted in several newspapers from Boston to Philadelphia, though nowhere south of the Potomac. It was his last public act. Three weeks later, on April 17, the founding grandfather finally went to his Maker.

Even prior to his passing, however, the great weight of Franklin's unequivocal endorsement of emancipation, even more his deft dismemberment of the proslavery posture of the deep south, made itself felt in the congressional debates. Smith of South Carolina attempted to discredit Franklin's views, observing that "even great men have their senile moments." But this prompted reprisals from the Pennsylvania delegation. "Instead of proving him superannuated," observed Thomas Scott, Franklin's pamphlet revealed "qualities of mind and soul yet in their vigor." Indeed, "only Franklin seemed to speak the language of America, and call us back to our first principles," thereby revealing that "an advocate for slavery at this stage of the world, and on the floor of the Congress too, is a phenomenon in politics that defied all belief." Scott's speech, which went on for over an hour, turned out to be the high-water mark of the antislavery effort in the House.[31]

o o o

Franklin's last piece of advice to his country was that slavery must be put on the national agenda before it was too late to take decisive action in accord with the core principles of the American Revolution, which were already fading into the middle distance. Although Madison had been uncharacteristically quiet during the debate over Franklin's legacy, he let it be known within the Virginia delegation that he agreed with Franklin's goals, but disagreed with his timing. To be sure, "slavery is a moral and political evil, and whatever brings forward some national and liberal plan for the gradual emancipation of slaves will deserve well of his country. Yet I think it was very improper at this time to introduce it in Congress." As he explained to Edmund Randolph, "The true policy of the southern members was to let the affair proceed with as little noise as possible." In effect, Franklin's followers were wrong to press the issue on one side, and the delegates from South Carolina and Georgia were even more wrong to do their intemperate shouting from the other side.[32]

Any effort to locate the core of Madison's position on slavery, therefore, misses the point, which is that there was no core, except perhaps the conviction that the whole topic was taboo. As a result, he had developed a way of talking and writing about the problem that might be described as "enlightened obfuscation," or perhaps the "Virginia straddle." For example, consider the following Madisonian statement delivered during the debate in the House: "If this folly did not reproach the public councils, it ought to excite no retort in the patrons of humanity and freedom. Nothing could hasten more the progress and sentiments which are secretly misinforming the institutions which this mistaken zeal is laboring to secure against the most distant approval of danger." The convoluted syntax, multiple negatives, indefinite antecedents, and masterful circumlocutions defy comprehension. What begins as a denunciation of those defending slavery somehow doubles back on itself and ends up in worrisome confusion that the matter is being talked about at all. What is meant to sound like an argument against slavery transforms itself in mid-passage into a verbal fog bank that descends over the entire subject like a cloud.[33]

On the face of it, Madison should have been pleased with the committee report, not because it was conveniently incoherent, but because it recommended that slavery be taken off the national agenda. There were two clarifying resolutions. The first resolution confirmed, "The Constitution prohibited any federal legislation limiting or ending the slave trade until 1808." The second resolution declared, "The Congress, by a fair construction of the Constitution, are equally restrained from interfering in the emancipation of slaves, who already are, or who may, within the period mentioned, be imported into or born within the said states."[34]

The key words in the second resolution were "within the period mentioned." In effect, the committee report extended the deadline for any consideration of emancipation to bring it into line with the deadline for the end of the slave trade. The deep south would get its way, but only for a limited time. After 1808, Congress possessed the authority to do whatever it wished. The deferral strategy had a clear time limit.

After the House went into committee-of-the-whole format to revise the language of the report, the Madisonian magic began to cast its spell. In parliamentary maneuverings of this sort, Madison had no peer. (If the gods were in the details, Madison was always poised to greet them upon arrival.) The Virginia delegation had already received its marching orders to mobilize behind an amended version of the second resolution. And several northern delegations, chiefly those from Massachusetts and New York, had been lobbied to support the amendment, which now read: "The Congress have no authority to interfere in the emancipation of slaves, or in Treatment of them within any of the states; it remaining with the several states alone to provide any realization therein."[35]

The final report passed by the House placed any congressional debate over slavery in the southern states out of bounds forever. What had begun as an initiative to put slavery on the road to extinction had been transformed into a decision to extinguish all federal plans for emancipation. It was the South Carolina solution achieved in the Virginia style. By a close vote of twenty-nine to twenty-five, the House transcribed its verdict into the permanent record, where it became a precedent with the status of common law.*

For example, when another Quaker petition came forward in 1792, William Loughton Smith referred his colleagues to the debate of 1790, observing that the House had then decided never again to allow itself to become inflamed by "the mere rant and rhapsody of a meddling fanatic," and concluding, "The subject would never be stirred again." The petition was withdrawn. More than forty years later, in 1833, Daniel Webster cited the same precedent: "My opinion is that Congress has no authority to interfere in the emancipation of slaves. This was resolved by the House in 1790, and I do not know of a different opinion since." Even Abraham Lincoln, when campaigning for the presidency in 1860, acknowledged that, although he had the legal authority to prohibit slavery in the incoming territories, he lacked the authority to tamper with slavery in the existent southern states.[36]

Whatever window of opportunity had existed to complete the most glaring piece of unfinished business in the revolutionary era was now closed. But the debate itself did not die. It moved from the political arena to the churches, where slavery would come under scrutiny as a sin requiring a national purging, and where the oral debate would not be burdened by realistic political considerations about the possible dismemberment of the emerging American republic. From a purely moral perspective, if that was the price to pay for salvation, so be it.

The political priorities of virtually all the prominent founders forbade such reasoning. Slavery was certainly an evil, but it was a necessary evil that must be endured for twenty years. The Madisonian maneuver had transformed twenty years into forever, had suc-

* Despite the legal precedent, however, several of those who had been delegates at the Constitutional Convention, including Washington, retained the conviction that the moratorium on slavery ended in 1808.

ceeded by a narrow margin and become settled law, one of the most consequential behind-the-scenes political maneuvers in American history. Hindsight allows us to know that "forever" now meant seventy years, and the final purging required the bloodiest war in American history.

One can only speculate what thoughts were streaking through the conscience of James Madison on April 22, when he was chosen to deliver the final tribute to the recently deceased Benjamin Franklin in the House. For Madison understood better than most what was at stake in the debate over slavery. He also knew what the American Revolution had promised, that slavery violated that promise, and that Franklin had gone to his Maker reminding all concerned that silence was a betrayal of the revolutionary legacy. Madison's eulogy merits inclusion in our list of unpainted scenes of the American founding:

> The House being informed of the decease of BENJAMIN FRANK-
> LIN, a citizen whose native genius was not more an Ornament
> to human nature than his various exertions of it have been pre-
> cious to science, to freedom, and to his country, do resolve, as
> a mark of the veneration due to his memory, that the members
> wear the customary badge of mourning for one month.[37]

The symbolism of the scene was poignant, dramatizing as it did the passing of both the prototypical American and the realistic prospects for placing slavery on the road to extinction. The badge of mourning the members of the House agreed to wear also bore testimony to the now tragic fate awaiting more than three generations of enslaved African Americans, and to what must be judged the greatest failure of the revolutionary generation.

o o o

The following chart is not a painting, but it is a printed picture of the enslaved population in 1790 based on the first census, which Congress authorized in order to provide accurate figures for determining the size of state delegations in the House. The category "All Other Free Persons" refers to Blacks.

*1790 Census of the United States**

STATES	FREE WHITE	ALL OTHER FREE PERSONS	SLAVES	TOTAL
Vermont	85,268	255	16	85,539
New Hampshire	141,097	630	158	141,885
Maine	96,002	538	none	96,540
Massachusetts	373,324	5,463	none	378,787
Rhode Island	64,470	3,407	948	68,825
Connecticut	232,674	2,808	2,764	237,946
New York	314,142	4,654	21,324	340,120
New Jersey	169,954	2,762	11,423	184,139
Pennsylvania	424,099	6,537	3,737	434,373
Delaware	46,310	3,899	8,887	59,094
Maryland	208,649	8,043	103,036	319,728
Virginia	442,117	12,866	292,627	747,610
Kentucky	61,133	114	12,430	73,677
North Carolina	288,204	4,975	100,572	393,751
South Carolina	140,178	1,801	107,094	249,073
Georgia	52,886	398	29,264	82,548
Total	3,140,205	59,150	694,280	3,893,635

* Data excerpted from U.S. Bureau of Census, *First Census of the United States* (Baltimore, 1978), 6–8.

At the most obvious level, the numbers confirmed with enhanced precision that slavery was a sectional problem that was dying slowly in the northern states and flourishing south of the Potomac. The exception to this rule was the upper south, where the slave populations of Maryland, Virginia, and North Carolina were large, but so was the populations of free Blacks. In fact, Virginia contained more free Blacks than any state in the union.

The sheer size of Virginia's total population, amplified by the daunting racial ratio, then further amplified by the political prowess of its leadership at the national level, all combined to make it the key state. If any plan to end slavery in the new nation were to succeed, Virginia needed to be in the vanguard. The leadership of prominent Virginians, especially Washington, Jefferson, and Madison, therefore became especially essential. None of them, it turned out, was up to the task, though Washington left a leadership legacy in his will.

The numbers for Kentucky were quite small, but they carried large and troubling implications. Kentucky, in fact, was still a territory, but it was the bellwether territory for all the looming territories of the southwest. As we have seen, there was an unspoken understanding during the debate over the Northwest Ordinance that prohibiting slavery in the Northwest Territories was conditional upon endorsing slavery in the Southwest Territories when they entered the union. The Kentucky numbers exposed the demographic fact that any sectional understanding was almost beside the point, because the importation of slaves from Virginia could not be stopped. The same pattern applied to Tennessee and Alabama, as extensions of the Carolinas and Georgia. To the extent that ending slavery required blocking its westward expansion, that battle was already well on its way to being lost.[38]

Finally, the census of 1790 provided unmistakable evidence that those antislavery advocates who believed that the future was on their side were deluding themselves. The slave population was now approaching seven hundred thousand, up from five hundred thousand in 1776. Despite the temporary end of the slave trade during the war, and despite the steady march of abolition in the north, the slave population was growing exponentially. Given the political and financial realities that defined the parameters of any comprehensive program for emancipation, chiefly compensation for owners and the relocation of freed slaves, the larger the enslaved population grew, the more impractical—indeed, daunting—any emancipation scheme became. The window of opportunity to end slavery was not opening, but closing.

Looking ahead, and switching the metaphor, several nails were hammered into the coffin of abolition over the next twenty years: the Haitian insurrection (1791–93); the cotton gin (1794); the domination of the presidency by the Virginia Dynasty, all defenders of states' rights over domestic policy (1800–1824); the Missouri Compromise (1820).

My contention is that these nails sealed shut the coffin containing a body that was already dead. Not only were the numbers becoming wholly unmanageable, but, the further one got from 1776, the lower the revolutionary fires burned, and the less imperative the values of the revolutionary promise seemed. In effect, the fading revolutionary ideology and the exploding racial demography were converging to close off all realistic options to end slavery where the vast majority of slaves resided. With all the advantages of hindsight, a persuasive case can be made that the Quaker petitioners, with a final gesture of preternatural wisdom from Benjamin Franklin, had called for a decisive action against slavery at the last possible moment when it had any meaningful prospect for success.

Chapter 7

The Treaty

۰ ۰ ۰

If we persist in the current policy, any idea of the Indian on this side of the Mississippi will only be found in the pages of the historian.

—HENRY KNOX, 1789

O N THE FACE of it, the biggest loser in the American war for independence was Great Britain, which lost most of its North American empire. But Great Britain rebounded from this devastating defeat to become the dominant world power for the following century and a half. Before history finally happened to the British Empire, its projection of imperial power around the globe enjoyed a level of success not seen since the headiest days of Rome. In that sense, the American Revolution was only a disappointing first act, followed by unparalleled British ascendancy.

There was no second act for the Native American population. For the roughly hundred thousand Indians living between the Appalachians and the Mississippi, the American victory in 1783 proved an unmitigated calamity from which history would provide no rescue, unless their forced removal to land west of the Mississippi can be regarded as such. The British defeat triggered a tidal wave of western migration on the part of settlers who understood the phrase "pursuit of happiness" to mean owning their own land. This demographic surge into Indian Country proved relentless and ultimately unstoppable. If only in retrospect, after the American Revolution the Indian population east of the Mississippi was fighting a holding action against the odds—ultimately, it was a matter of numbers—in which the tragic conclusion seems to have been inevitable.[1]

But the clairvoyance of hindsight actually obscures the choices perceived by the participants caught in the moment. On the Indian side, it never occurred to most tribal chiefs that the scratch of a pen in Paris had dispossessed them of lands they had controlled for centuries. The British intruders had now been replaced by the American intruders, to be sure, but there seemed no reason to believe that this change would mean that the future would be dramatically different from the past. The exception, and a major one, was the Iroquois Confederacy, called the Six Nations, whose alliance with Great Britain had cost them dearly during the war, a devastating experience that allowed them to glimpse the inexorable power building to the east. For the more western tribes, on the other hand, in that vast expanse stretching south from the Ohio Valley through what is now Tennessee, Alabama, and Mississippi, the war between the Whites remained a distant event of little consequence for their daily lives. Until the front edge of the looming American invasion reached their tribal lands, most Indian leaders presumed, quite plausibly, that what one Shawnee chief called "our island" was both safe and impregnable. Nothing in their previous experience equipped them to regard themselves as tragic victims.[2]

Meanwhile, on the American side, the leadership of the new national government created by the recently ratified Constitution declared its determination to avoid a policy of Indian removal at almost any cost. Under the Articles of Confederation, Indian policy had been an incoherent blend of federal and state jurisdictions, with a gloss of reassuring rhetoric that covered a crude reality of outright confiscation. Now, for the first time, the power to implement a coherent national policy toward the Indian tribes east of the Mississippi was vested in the federal government and, more specifically, in the executive branch. This effectively placed control of policy in the hands of three people: President George Washington, Secretary of State Thomas Jefferson, and Secretary of War Henry Knox. All three agreed on two fundamental principles: first, Indian policy was a branch of foreign policy, or, as Knox put it, "the independent tribes of Indians ought to be considered as foreign nations, not as the subjects of any particular state," a position that sanctioned federal authority over the states and executive authority over policy making; second, as sovereign nations, the Indian tribes possessed legitimate rights that must be respected. Again, Knox put it most succinctly: "Indians being the prior occupants of the rights of the soil . . . to dispossess them . . . would be a gross violation of the fundamental Laws of Nature and of that distributive Justice which is the glory of a nation."[3]

In short, as the apparently inevitable tragedy so clear to us began to unfold, neither side regarded it as inevitable. Washington went so far as to declare that a truly just Indian policy was one of his highest priorities, that failure on this score would damage his reputation and "stain the nation." No man in American history was more accustomed to getting his way than Washington, especially when he invested his personal prestige in the cause. The fate of the Native American population proved the exception to that rule, a case where his own efforts proved inadequate for reasons that not even he could control.[4]

This, then, is a story about failure. Next to the failure to end slavery, or at least put it on the road to extinction, the inability to reach a just accommodation with the Native Americans was the greatest failure of the revolutionary generation. And they knew it. Here the creative response to a daunting challenge, a capacity that had risen to the occasion in earlier crises, proved inadequate to the task at hand. Perhaps the problem was insoluble. But, then, harnessing the radical impulses of the Revolution, defeating the most powerful military force in the world, and forging a union among thirteen sovereignties had all appeared insoluble as well. And some combination of imagination, vigorous commitment, pragmatic adjustments, and dumb luck had won the day. Not so on this occasion.

"Why?" is an intriguing question, rendered even more interesting because all the major white players in the story—Washington, Jefferson, and Knox—believed that a solution was quite clear, at least theoretically. But the real star of the story was a charismatic, mixed-blood Creek chief named Alexander McGillivray, who became the one-man embodiment of the answer to the entire dilemma. McGillivray's designation as the singular solution was, at least in retrospect, an act of desperation for which he should not be judged accountable. Despite being the most talented Indian statesman of his time, McGillivray lacked the power to avert the tragic outcome. And, as Washington eventually discovered, he himself lacked the power as well. The power did not reside in political leaders or even in government itself. Ultimate power lay with those white settlers streaming over the Appalachians into Indian Country, a relentless tide that swept all treaties, promises, excellent intentions, and moral considerations to the far banks of history. This, then, is a story about irony, in which the triumph of the American people made an American tragedy inevitable for the first Americans. In the end, demography trumped diplomacy.[5]

o o o

No Indians were present for the negotiation of the Treaty of Paris. On the one hand, this was wholly understandable, since the multiple tribes were not nation-states in the manner of Great Britain, France, and the United States, so it is difficult to imagine which tribes or confederation of tribes deserved a place at the table. On the other hand, the treaty shifted control over the eastern third of North America from Britain to the United States, a landmass stretching from the Atlantic to the Mississippi and the Great Lakes to the Gulf of Mexico. Three-quarters of that huge area remained Indian Country, with a resident population of approximately thirty tribes long accustomed to regarding the land as their gift from the Great Spirit. It never occurred to them that this expansive region could be owned by any mortal, much less that control over land could shift because mere men an ocean away, who had never hunted or walked upon its ground, had written their names on a piece of parchment.

In truth, it also never occurred to the diplomats in Paris to invite Indian representatives to the negotiations. Throughout the colonial period, all the European powers presumed that the entire Western Hemisphere could be carved up among themselves based on decisions made in London, Paris, and Madrid, which in turn were based on previous explorations, subsequently rendered legal by kingly proclamations. For example, the French based their claim to the entire Mississippi Valley on La Salle's sail down the river in the seventeenth century. (They later buried lead plates along the banks to register their claim.) The British based their claim to the Ohio Country and beyond on the Virginia Charter of 1606, which had conveniently left the western border of the colony undefined, leaving lawyers to decide whether the proper boundary was the Mississippi or the Pacific Ocean.

The arrogance of this Eurocentric approach was matched only by its ignorance, since most of the European diplomats would have been hard-pressed to distinguish the Appalachians from the Rockies or the Mississippi from the Potomac. But, arrogance and ignorance aside, this imperious mode of defining empire enjoyed the incalculable advantage of being the unquestioned way of doing business within all the European capitals and courts. It was what being an empire was all about. Whether they realized it or not, by signing the Treaty of Paris, the newly created American republic was announcing its arrival as the youngest member of the imperial family and the successor to France and Great Britain as the sovereign power over all the people south of Canada and north of Florida.

This new imperial status raised for the first time a disquieting question that has haunted American foreign policy ever since. Put simply, how could a republic be an empire? More specifically, how could a government founded on the principles articulated in the Declaration of Independence, which stigmatized the arbitrary and coercive policies of the British Empire, then proceed to behave just as imperiously toward the original occupants of American soil as the British had acted toward them? More tellingly, did not the treatment of the Indian population constitute an obvious acid test of the republican values the American Revolution claimed to stand for?

Initially, from 1783 to 1786, the Confederation Congress and the commissioners they appointed to negotiate treaties with several Indian tribes preferred not to notice the contradiction. Treaties signed with the Six Nations at Fort Stanwix, with the Ohio tribes at Ford McIntosh, and with the Cherokees at Hopewell were blatantly imperialistic affairs in which the American negotiators argued that the Indians were "a conquered people" who should be grateful to be consulted at all: "You are mistaken in supposing that . . . you have become a free and independent nation," explained one American negotiator, "and can make what terms as you please. It is not so. You are a subdued people."[6]

As the Americans saw the situation, after the Treaty of Paris there was no such thing as Indian Country, since all the land from the Atlantic to the Mississippi belonged to the United States by right of conquest. When the chiefs of the Ohio tribes expressed their willingness to negotiate concerning lands south of the Ohio

River, the American commissioners corrected them: "We claim the country by conquest; and you are to give not to receive." It was a take-it-or-leave-it proposition in which the Indians surrendered a portion of their tribal lands or faced war with the United States.[7]

From the very start, however, this explicit expression of American power struck some observers as too conspicuously coercive. Not only did the conquest theory make the United States appear to be just another imperial power in the European mode, it almost surely entailed a series of Indian wars on the frontier that would prove expensive in blood and treasure. (And events were to demonstrate that the Ohio tribes were a much more formidable enemy than anyone had initially imagined.) An alternative approach was first proposed by Philip Schuyler, a former general in the Continental Army and prominent New York land baron who had extensive experience dealing with the Six Nations during the war.

Schuyler's proposal envisioned a more gradual and indirect form of American imperialism. Rather than take the eastern third of the continent in one gulp, he recommended a series of smaller bites, a staged expansion driven by the front edge of American settlements. "As our settlements approach their country," Schuyler explained, "they [Indians] must, from the scarcity of game, retire further back, and dispose of their lands, until they dwindle comparatively to nothing, as all savages have done . . . when compelled to live in the vicinity of civilized people." The end would be the same—eventual Indian removal east of the Mississippi—but the means would be less violent and blatant, because demography would do the work of armies. In the Schuyler scheme, the Americans could afford to be patient and gracious at each stage, knowing full well that every treaty was merely a temporary halt on the inexorable march westward. From a republican point of view, the great advantage of this strategy was to replace outright coercion with some semblance of mutual consent. One might call it veiled imperialism, or perhaps imperialism without an imperious edge—a more cost-effective and palatable version of genocide that permitted republican principles to coexist, albeit uneasily, alongside Indian extinction.[8]

Within the Confederation Congress, there was little dissent about the proper direction of Indian policy—staged removal—but considerable confusion about who should manage it. Congress enacted an ordinance in August 1786 giving itself "the sole and exclusive right . . . of regulating the trade and managing the affairs with the Indians, not members of any states." This seemed clear enough, and sanctioned a congressional provision creating northern and southern departments of Indian affairs above and below the Ohio River that reported to the secretary of war, an ominous sign that diplomacy would probably not suffice. But in the same ordinance the Confederation Congress qualified its own claim to jurisdiction by declaring that federal authority only obtained "provided that the legislative right of any state within its own limits be not infringed or violated." This language seemed to sanction the separate treaties that New York, North Carolina, and Georgia were negotiating with Indian tribes within their borders, creating constitutional confusion about who was really in charge.[9]

A different kind of mixed message was sent in the Northwest Ordinance of 1787. On the one hand, the ordinance defined the terms for establishing territories and soon-to-be states in the region stretching from the Ohio River to the Mississippi. The clear implication of this landmark legislation was that any Indian presence in the northwest was presumed to be temporary, despite treaty obligations with the Ohio tribes that said otherwise. On the other hand, the ordinance also contained a reassuring promise that American policy toward the Indians would always be conducted according to the purest version of republican principles:

> The utmost good faith shall always be observed towards the Indians; their lands and property shall never be taken from

them without their consent; and in their property, rights, and liberty, they shall never be invaded or disturbed, unless by just and lawful wars authorized by Congress; but laws founded on justice and humanity, shall, from time to time, be made, for preventing wrongs being done to them. . . .

Whether this rhetorical flourish was designed to mislead the Indians or to soothe the consciences of its American authors, or some subtle combination of the two, is impossible to know. Given the relentless reality of the ongoing removal policy, however, it is difficult to avoid the conclusion that such promises of justice constituted a republican cloak over an imperialistic agenda.[10]

Just a few months after he assumed office as president, George Washington received a rather remarkable letter from Henry Knox, his recently appointed secretary of war. Federal authority over Indian policy needed to be clarified, Knox argued, in order to rescue it from the jurisdictional confusion that had prevailed under the Articles of Confederation. The best way to achieve the necessary clarity, Knox suggested, was to insist that "the independent tribes of Indians ought to be considered as foreign nations, not as the subjects of any particular state." Although the recently ratified Constitution had very little to say about Indians or Indian policy, one phrase (Article 1, Section 8) authorized Congress "to regulate commerce with foreign nations, and among the several states, and with the Indian tribes."

This language provided ample grounds for claiming federal sovereignty over the states, and insisting that all Indian tribes were foreign nations and that all treaties with them fell under the authority of the executive branch to make treaties "with the advice and consent of the Senate" (Article 2, Section 2). The ink on the Constitution was barely dry, but Knox was engaging in a pioneering effort—the effort continues apace today—to interpret the meaning of its words. In this instance, the goal was to lodge control over Indian policy squarely in the executive branch of the federal government.[11]

But Knox was just getting started. Once the executive branch achieved jurisdiction, he argued that virtually all the premises on which Indian policy had previously been conducted required review. The conquest theory, which presumed that all Indians east of the Mississippi were mere "tenants at will," struck Knox as a gross violation of the republican principles that he and Washington had fought for in the last war. "It would reflect honor on the new government," Knox observed, "were a declarative Law to be passed that the Indian tribes possess the right of the soil of all lands . . . and that they are not to be divested thereof but in consequence of fair and bona fide purchases, made under the authority, or with the express approbation of the United States." There were matters of principle at stake here with long-term implications for both the fate of the Indians and the fate of the republican experiment itself. Knox was saying that, as the chief symbol and custodian of the revolutionary legacy, Washington needed to recognize that his own place in history would be considerably influenced by his management of this crucial issue at this most propitious moment.[12]

What, for example, might posterity say if, "instead of exterminating a part of the human race by our modes of population"—which is to say the demographic strategy of Indian removal—"we had persevered through all difficulties and at last had imparted our Knowledge of cultivation, and the arts, to the Aboriginals of the Country?" What, on the other hand, would posterity say "if we persist in the current policy, which is in truth to assure that in a short period the Idea of the Indian on this side of the Mississippi will only be found in the pages of the historian?"[13]

Knox was recommending a wholesale reversal of American Indian policy, in effect arguing that a genuine republic could not function in the manner of European empires. Not only did the conquest theory violate republican principles, but the demographic strategy of removal was only an oblique version of imperialism, a more gradual and palatable version of removal. Knox was challenging the legacy and morality of removal itself—the fundamental assumption of American Indian policy no matter how achieved. This was a stunning suggestion, even more radical in that no government official to date had dared even to mention an alternative scenario. Knox was arguing that the prevailing policy of the United States toward Native Americans was nothing less than a direct repudiation of the values embodied in the American Revolution.[14]

Throughout the summer of 1789, Knox lobbied Washington to make reform of American Indian policy a priority of his presidency. It is difficult to know which of Knox's arguments—the moral, the economic, or the fate of Washington's reputation—had the greatest impact. Clearly, Knox managed to capture Washington's attention and persuade him to rethink his earlier position on Indian policy, which had presumed the inevitability and desirability of removal. This itself was a major achievement, since Washington was simultaneously preoccupied with appointments to his Cabinet, defining the intentionally vague powers of his office as described in the Constitution, delegating fiscal policy to Alexander Hamilton, and in general launching the first large-scale experiment in republican government in all history. For Washington to decide that Indian affairs merited his personal attention amid this cacophony of political and constitutional pressures was a testimony to Knox's influence and to Washington's recognition that the issue at stake was too important to be delegated to others.

Knox and Washington hammered out the shape of a new Indian policy for the United States in the late summer of 1789. Strictly speaking, once the Indian tribes were defined as foreign nations, Indian policy should have become a branch of foreign policy under the authority of the secretary of state. But Thomas Jefferson, recently appointed to that office, was on the way home from

Paris, and domestic affairs—the marriage of his eldest daughter—would delay his arrival in the capital at New York until the following spring. Since Knox had essentially been doing the job for the past three years anyway, had all the relevant information at his fingertips, and in fact was the primary advocate for a basic change in American policy, Jefferson's absence made little difference, and might actually have helped the cause, since it would have taken time to bring Jefferson up to speed.

The presumptive inequality inherent in the conquest theory would be replaced by treaties between equals negotiated "on principles consistent with the national justice and dignity of the United States." Coercion, the imperial way of doing business, would be replaced by mutual consent, the republican way. The terms of all treaties would be binding on both parties in perpetuity, and both the power and the honor of the federal government would be pledged to their enforcement. The demographic version of Indian removal would be strenuously opposed, if necessary, by American troops garrisoned on the borders of Indian Country to block white migration and evict any settlers who managed to elude their surveillance. All treaties would also contain a provision whereby the tribes would be provided with tools and instruction in husbandry so that they could make a gradual transition from hunting and gathering to agricultural economies, which would simultaneously allow Indian culture to evolve to a more civilized status and reduce the size of the territory necessary for Indian survival.

What Knox and Washington envisioned as the outcome of the new policy was a series of Indian enclaves or homelands east of the Mississippi, whose political and geographic integrity would be protected by federal law. The wave of white settlements would be required to bypass these Indian enclaves, leaving several Indian territories east of the Mississippi that would eventually, over the course of the next century, be assimilated as new states. It was a vision in which the westward expansion of an American empire coexisted alongside the preservation of the original Americans.[15]

But would it work? The only way to find out was to try it, the only question being what tribe or confederation of tribes to select as the ideal test case. Knox, in fact, had already made that decision. In July 1789, he began sending Washington extensive reports on the Creek Nation, whose hunting grounds extended from western Georgia to northern Florida and across modern Alabama into eastern Mississippi. The Creeks were a southern version of the Iroquois, in the sense that they exercised considerable influence over adjoining tribes, including the Cherokees to the north and the Chickasaws and Choctaws to the south and west, so that a treaty with the Creeks had broader implications for the entire southern department. What's more, the Creeks were already well on their way to developing an agricultural economy, one reason they and their tribal neighbors were referred to as the "Civilized Tribes." Their economy had become dependent on obtaining supplies (tools, clothing, blankets, weapons) from British agents in Pensacola and Spanish agents in New Orleans. If the United States could displace the British and Spanish as their major trading partner, political allegiance was sure to follow. Finally, there was a dominant chief in the Creek Nation, Alexander McGillivray, who exercised near-dictatorial authority over all Creek tribal councils. Unlike the Ohio tribes, where authority was divided among several warrior-chiefs, the Creeks had an acknowledged leader who could speak for their nation and enforce the terms of a treaty dependably. All in all, if the experiment required a laboratory, the Creeks seemed to present the optimal opportunity for success.

By late August 1789, Knox had persuaded Washington to draft a model treaty with the Creeks based on the new approach. Because this would be the first treaty with a foreign power negotiated since the ratification of the Constitution, it forced Washington to inter-

pret the constitutional requirement to obtain "the advice and consent of the Senate" for the first time. Washington believed that the
phrase required him to consult with the Senate in person, so he
scheduled a meeting in the Senate for August 22, accompanied by
Knox.

The result was part fiasco, part comedy. Because this was a
precedent-setting occasion, the Senate spent most of the previous
day debating parliamentary etiquette, including where the president
should sit and whether or not to applaud his entrance. The following day, Washington presented the case for sending a commission
to the Creeks with treaty terms designed "to attach them firmly to
the United States" and thereby put an end to the sporadic violence
on the southern frontier. Washington blamed the bulk of the violence on the Georgians rather than the Creeks, claiming that the
borders established by previous treaties "have been entirely violated
by the disorderly white people on the frontiers." But, regardless of
the question of culpability, it was now time to reach a new and just
accommodation with the southern tribes, and the proposed treaty
with the Creeks would begin that important diplomatic process. If
the members of the Senate had any specific questions, Secretary of
War Knox would be pleased to answer them.[16]

Then the farce began. Several senators declared that they could
not possibly provide their advice and consent until they had seen all
the relevant documents. Knox's explanations were surely accurate,
but hardly adequate; they needed to see for themselves. Other senators suggested that, given the need to review the documents, perhaps the best way to proceed was to refer the matter to a committee.
Senator William Maclay of Pennsylvania reported that Washington became visibly irritated and was heard to mutter, "This defeats
every purpose of my coming here." Once the senators realized that
they had given offense to the president, they became reluctant to
speak, producing several awkward silences. Washington eventually
got up, motioned toward Knox to follow him, and strode out of the

Senate "with a discontented air" and vowing under his breath never to return.[17]

He broke that vow two days later. This time, he provided the Senate with three written-out questions beforehand. There was no debate. The Senate, properly embarrassed about the awkwardness of the previous session, endorsed the appointment of a special commission to negotiate a treaty with the Creeks. Washington thanked the Senate, walked out briskly, and never returned; from that moment to the present day, "the advice and consent of the Senate" ceased to mean direct presidential consultation.

The instructions to the commissioners, drafted by Knox, urged them "by a just and liberal system of policy to conciliate and attach them [i.e., the Creeks] to the Interests of the union." If any of the previous treaties were found to be faulty, the commissioners were instructed to renegotiate them and pay compensation for past misunderstandings. They should promise to place the Creek Nation "under the protection of the United States of America," to include a line of military posts to guarantee the new borders against white encroachments. Finally, the commissioners should establish a bond of trust with Alexander McGillivray, who "was reputed to possess great abilities and unlimited influence over the Creek nation and part of the Cherokees." Winning over McGillivray was the highest priority, and, in order to "attach him warmly to the United States," they were permitted to offer him military rank in the American army with its attendant salary in return for an oath of loyalty. This thinly veiled bribe should do the trick. They had no way of knowing that they were dealing with the Talleyrand of the southern frontier.[18]

० ० ०

The commission sent to offer McGillivray the opportunity to launch a new chapter in Indian-American relations on the Knox model was headed by Benjamin Lincoln, one of Washington's favorite generals during the Revolutionary War. Lincoln was accompanied by David Humphreys, a former aide-de-camp to Washington with a degree from Yale, the ambition to become a major American poet, diplomatic experience in Europe, and bottomless confidence in his own significance. Knox had stacked the commission with men of stature whom he and Washington knew personally. The negotiations designed to establish a fundamentally new direction in American Indian policy were scheduled for late September at a frontier outpost named Rock Landing, which was located in what is now central Georgia, on disputed land between the Ogeechee and Oconee Rivers. McGillivray, leaving nothing to chance, arrived accompanied by an entourage of nine hundred Creek warriors and chiefs.

All descriptions of McGillivray that have survived agree on two points: he was light-skinned and physically unimpressive. The light skin was a function of his mixed ancestry. His father was a well-to-do Scotsman who had sided with the British in the late war, had his estate confiscated along with other loyalists, then sailed home to Scotland, never to return. His mother was half French and half Creek, making McGillivray only one-quarter Indian. But because Creek society was matrilineal, and his mother was descended from a prominent Creek family, McGillivray was regarded by all the Creeks as a full-blooded member of the Creek Nation.[19]

Physically, he was a walking bundle of ailments. He suffered from migraine headaches and acute rheumatism that often incapacitated him for weeks at a time. He also labored under several self-inflicted diseases, including chronic alcoholism and syphilis sufficiently severe that his fingernails kept falling out. Unlike that of most Indian chiefs, McGillivray's stature did not depend on his conspicuous bravery in battle. He himself acknowledged that he was not much of a warrior, and that in his first engagement he had hidden behind a bush during the fighting, then crawled out at night to take the scalp of a dead American soldier.

His prowess as a Creek leader derived from his intellectual rather than physical strengths. His father had sent him to Charleston to receive a classical education in Latin and Greek. McGillivray was fluent in English, Spanish, and Creek, and well read in British and European history. When most Indian chiefs were confronted with the conquest explanation for their loss of standing after the Treaty of Paris, they could respond only with a mixture of confusion and disbelief. McGillivray denounced the conquest theory as a violation of international law:

> We do in the most solemn manner protest against any title claim or Demand the American Congress may set up for our lands, Settlements, and hunting Grounds in Consequence of the Said treaty of peace between the King of Great Britain and the States of America, declaring that we were not partys, it being a Notorious fact known to the Americans, known to every person who is in any ways conversant in, or acquainted with American affairs, that his Brittanick Majesty was never possessed either by session purchase or by right of Conquest of our Terrirorys and which the Said treaty gives away.

In short, no one—neither the British nor the Americans—had ever conquered the Creeks, so the entire conquest argument was really a transparent rationale for outright thievery.[20]

McGillivray's control over the Upper Creek and Lower Creek tribes, as well as his influence over their Cherokee, Chickasaw, and Choctaw neighbors, was rooted in his literacy in English and Spanish and his impressive negotiating skills with British and Spanish traders, who provided tools, clothing, weaponry, and amenities to all the southern tribes. All licenses to trade with the various tribes required his authorization, for which he collected a fee. He was also part owner of the major trading post in Pensacola, which earned him a handsome annual profit and allowed him to amass the wealth of an Indian-styled southern aristocrat. He owned a log mansion, fifty to sixty slaves, and several hundred horses and cattle in Little Tallahassee, near present-day Montgomery, Alabama. He also owned a smaller plantation, with another wife and family, in Mobile.

He defied all the stereotypes: part Indian, part White; part defender of Creek rights, part southern slaveowner; part statesman, part corrupt power broker. An unalloyed realist, McGillivray regarded the building wave of white settlers on his eastern borders as the greatest threat. For that reason, amid all his multiple identities, he was resolutely anti-American.

As a result, McGillivray was extremely reluctant to attend the conference at Rock Landing. As he saw it, the balance of power in the region belonged to the Creek Nation and its allies. He could deploy over five thousand warriors at a moment's notice, a force more than sufficient to defeat any attack by Georgia's militia. And the puny American army was tied down in ongoing battles with the Ohio tribes. As long as Spanish supplies flowed freely to his warriors, Creek Country was impregnable. What's more, he did not trust the word of the Americans. His contacts with the Six Nations and the Ohio tribes made him fully aware that all treaties with the Americans establishing secure borders had almost immediately been violated. And his own experience with the state governments of South Carolina and Georgia only reinforced his skepticism: "We have received friendly talks and replies, it is true," he observed, "but while they are addressing us by the flattering appellations of Friends and Brothers, they are stripping us of our natural rights by depriving us of that inheritance which belonged to our ancestors and hath descended from them to us Since the beginning of time."[21]

Ironically, he was persuaded to attend the conference with the

Americans by Esteban Miró, the Spanish governor of Louisiana. Miró obviously did not want McGillivray to sign a treaty with the Americans, but he feared that an unwillingness to negotiate would lead to a full-scale war on the southern frontier. McGillivray believed that the Creeks could win such a war, but Miró was less confident; he feared that an American victory might mean Spain lost all of Florida, which at the time included the entire Gulf Coast. Since McGillivray could not afford to alienate his Spanish allies, he agreed to show up at Rock Landing. The diplomatic chemistry was therefore poisoned from the start. The American commissioners believed that they were launching a new era in Indian affairs destined to establish a precedent for Indian-White coexistence east of the Mississippi. McGillivray believed that he was jumping through the proverbial hoops, appeasing the American negotiators, pretending to be pliable, drawing out the inevitable confrontation.

Humphreys, who did the bulk of the negotiating on the American side, had a somewhat mixed first impression of McGillivray: "His countenance has nothing liberal and open in it—it has however sufficient marks of understanding. In short, he appears to have the good sense of an American, the shrewdness of a Scotchman & the cunning of an Indian. . . . His influence is probably as great as we have understood it was." Meanwhile, McGillivray's first impression of Humphreys was totally negative. He described Humphreys as "that puppy" and "a great boaster of his political knowledge," a mere babe in the woods whose presumptive tone and condescending style were almost too much to bear.[22]

The treaty terms Humphreys proposed were also a problem. From Humphreys's perspective, he was offering the Creeks the most generous terms ever made to any Indian tribe, a guarantee of almost all their tribal land and a promise of protection by the federal government against white encroachments. From McGillivray's perspective, the proposed treaty required the Creeks to surrender their claim to the land between the Ogeechee and Oconee Rivers, where several hundred white families were already settled. When Humphreys pointed out that the disputed land had already been surrendered to Georgia in a previous treaty, McGillivray argued that he never had agreed and never would agree to give up any Creek land, and that the Georgians had found some "Indian vagabond" who lacked any authority to sign that treaty, which was clearly illegal. As for the American promise of protection, the Creek Nation did not require protection. It could perfectly well take care of itself and had no desire to become an American colony. And why should he trust American promises, given the undeniable record of broken promises with the Six Nations and the Ohio tribes?

Humphreys's version of what happened next emphasized McGillivray's obstinacy, fueled by huge consumption of whiskey. "He got very much intoxicated," Humphreys reported, though he also observed that McGillivray "seemed to retain his recollection and reason beyond what I had ever seen in a person, when in the same condition." McGillivray's version took pride in his intransigence: "The arts of flattery ambition and intimidation were exhausted in vain. I at last told him that by G   d I would not have such a Treaty cram'd down my throat . . . so I remained obstinate in my purpose and came on." By "came on" McGillivray meant that he gathered together his nine hundred warriors and rode out of Rock Landing.[23]

McGillivray left Rock Landing with spirits soaring. He had upheld the honor of the Creek people against the implicit coercion of the American government, which had the audacity to send a mere child-man to intimidate the chief of the Creek Nation. What stories he could now tell around the council campfires of American desperation and weakness. On the ride home, he encountered a group of Georgia settlers who requested his permission to carve out a colony of their own within Creek Country under his protection. McGillivray observed:

Although I am not a sorcerer, I could manage them as I pleased. They are extremely ignorant and unpolished; each sentence that came from my mouth, they took as pure gospel. They got it into their heads that I was going to establish a new state, and 1500 families were ready to present me with petitions to become my subjects. I amused myself and juggled with them until we parted.

If they did attempt to settle on Creek land, he would order his warriors to drive them away and, if they refused, "to kill every one of them."[24]

Knox apprised Washington that their best effort to forge a new Indian policy had failed miserably: "We have the Mortification to inform you that the Parties have separated without a Treaty. The terms which were offered . . . were not agreeable to Mr. McGillivray." Washington had just returned from a monthlong tour of New England and faced a backlog of pressing decisions, which included appointments to the newly created federal judiciary, preliminary discussions with Alexander Hamilton about the size of the national debt and the proper outlines for American fiscal policy, plus a steady barrage of letters from job applicants, many former veterans courting favor. But he pushed aside all these important chores to immerse himself completely in the correspondence and documents relating to the Creek problem. The entire future of American Indian policy was at stake. The northern frontier was on the verge of open warfare with the Ohio tribes. Now the southern frontier threatened to explode as well. This was an issue that required his undivided attention.[25]

What had begun as an initiative by Knox driven by a clear moral imperative—the preservation of Indian culture east of the Mississippi—was now transformed into a strategic dilemma driven by economic considerations. How many warriors could McGillivray deploy, how many federal troops would be required to defeat him, and what would the campaign cost? What was the likelihood of an alliance of all the southern tribes under McGillivray? And then—the nightmare scenario—what was the possibility of a pan-Indian alliance of all the northern and southern tribes, with McGillivray playing the leadership role that Pontiac, the great pan-Indian chief of the 1760s, had played earlier?[26]

The answers that Knox provided were not encouraging. An all-out war against the southern tribes would cost at least fifteen million dollars, based on the estimate that McGillivray could call upon five thousand warriors, or more if the Cherokees, Choctaws, and Chickasaws joined the campaign. Presuming that the Ohio tribes mounted an organized resistance that required a military response, the United States would be forced to fight a two-front war, the cost of which in men and money would defy the imagination.[27]

When they brought the same cost-benefit calculus to the combustible situation on the southern frontier, the conclusion was crystal clear. A military campaign against the Creeks was politically and economically impossible to justify; only a diplomatic solution made sense. And that meant that McGillivray must be appeased—not because doing so was morally right, but because it was now strategically necessary.

Then a new ingredient entered the strategic chemistry, an ingredient equally worrisome to McGillivray and the Washington-Knox tandem. In January 1790, the Georgia legislature announced the sale of twenty-four million acres of land to three private companies, collectively called the Yazoo companies, which claimed control over a vast region now comprising the states of Tennessee, Alabama, and Mississippi—in other words, all of Creek Country. The legal rationale for this sale was the original Georgia Charter, which placed the western border of the then colony at the Mississippi River. This inflated claim made perfect sense to most members of the Georgia legislature, who owned shares in this speculative bonanza, making it a thoroughly corrupt and breath-takingly brazen scheme from the start.[28]

From the perspective of Knox and Washington, this Yazoo initiative was a blatant assertion of state sovereignty that defied both the principle of federal control over Indian affairs and the prevailing presumption that Indian policy was a branch of American foreign policy. If allowed to stand, it made any treaty with the Creek Nation inherently worthless. From McGillivray's perspective, the Yazoo initiative threatened to release a gigantic new wave of white settlers into Creek Country, a demographic occupation more formidable than a conventional military invasion. He was confident he could defeat an American army, but endless waves of settlers posed the threat of an endless war on the southern frontier that even McGillivray could not be sure to win.

Because McGillivray had a well-earned reputation for unscrupulous behavior and had also demonstrated that he did not mind cutting deals that lined his own pockets on occasion, a delegation of Georgia stockholders in Yazoo attempted to bribe him by offering him shares in the lucrative venture in return for his cooperation. But McGillivray was unscrupulous only when it served the greater interests of the Creek Nation. He rejected the bribe and interpreted the offer as further evidence of his critical role as the dominant power broker on the southern frontier. He took even greater satisfaction in his obvious importance when he learned that, having failed to bribe him, several anonymous Georgia legislators had put out a contract to have him assassinated.[29]

This development altered the political chemistry. Prior to Yazoo, McGillivray would almost surely have rejected any offer from Knox and Washington to renew negotiations, convinced as he was that the Creeks and their Indian allies, handsomely supplied by Spain, controlled the balance of power in the region. Now, however, the resumption of negotiations would allow McGillivray to sign a treaty with the federal government that reaffirmed federal control over Indian policy and thereby undercut Georgia's preposterous claims of sovereignty. On this crucial point, his agenda and the Knox-Washington agenda were perfectly aligned.

Beyond that common point, however, McGillivray harbored no illusions. "All the eagerness which Washington shows to treat with me on such liberal terms," McGillivray observed, "is not based, I am persuaded, on principles of Justice and humanity." The Americans were already stretched too thin because of the ongoing war on the northern frontier and lacked sufficient manpower and money to mount a viable military campaign in the south. Their menacing threats on that score were only a bluff that he was fully prepared to call. But if he could negotiate a treaty that aligned the federal government with the Creek Nation against the Georgians, the Yazoo threat was likely to disappear.[30]

The new American offer was hand-delivered by a former officer in the Continental Army named Marinus Willett. Knox and Washington had decided to pull out all the stops. All matters, including the disputed land between the Ogeechee and Oconee Rivers, were on the table for negotiation. More significantly, McGillivray would not be required to deal with inferior underlings like Humphreys. This time the two great leaders, Washington and McGillivray, would meet at the summit. McGillivray and a delegation of lesser Creek chiefs were invited to the American capital at New York for an extended visit that would permit promises to be made face-to-face, in the best tradition of the Indian council fires.[31]

McGillivray found Willett more candid than Humphreys, a man of parts who might have made an excellent Creek warrior. Though McGillivray was immune to all forms of flattery and did not enjoy the prospects of a long and tiring trip, especially given his somewhat questionable physical stamina, this was an offer he could not refuse. "A treaty concluded at New York, ratified with the signature of Washington and McGillivray," he noted with obvious pride in the co-equal status, "would be the bond of Long Peace and revered by Americans to a distant period." He began making preparations for the seven-hundred-mile excursion in May 1790.[32]

o o o

It was quite a scene. McGillivray rode in a coach with his American escort, Marinus Willett, followed by twenty-seven Creek chiefs on horseback, all fully feathered and resplendent in Indian dress as they traveled toward the white man's capital. Witnesses along the roads in Georgia and the Carolinas were stunned, claiming they had never seen so many warriors whose intentions were entirely peaceful. In Virginia, there were mandatory stops in Richmond and Fredericksburg, where local dignitaries hosted lavish dinners, complete with multiple toasts to "the Creek Washington." Philadelphia provided an even greater extravaganza of celebration. By the time the procession reached the outskirts of New York, so many peace pipes had been smoked and so many glasses had been lifted that the diplomatic negotiations themselves seemed a ceremonial afterthought. The cheering crowds signaled the start of a new era of peace on the southern frontier.

As they were ferried across from New Jersey to Manhattan, McGillivray and his entourage were welcomed like European royalty. One New York newspaper claimed that they had seen nothing like it since Washington's inauguration. Ships in the harbor fired salutary salvos. Officers from the St. Tammany's Society greeted them at the wharf, clad in Indian bonnets as a statement of their fraternal fellowship. Then there was a parade past Federal Hall, and all the members of Congress came out to cheer while the Creek chiefs broke out in song that interpreters described as a tribute to brotherhood. The festive procession then moved to Knox's house, where Knox invited McGillivray to reside during his stay in New York and McGillivray announced that he would deposit his nephew to the care of the Knox family for his education and upbringing, which symbolized the union of the two families. Then it was on to the presidential mansion, where Washington offered his official welcome. The extravaganza ended at City Tavern with a sumptuous dinner and more toasts, all punctuated by Creek songs and shouts that gave the occasion an exotic flavor by blending Indian and white versions of etiquette. It was what we might call a major multicultural event.[33]

Coverage in the New York press concurred that no European diplomats had ever been welcomed so royally. As Knox and Washington saw it, this made perfect sense, since winning over McGillivray was more strategically crucial than solidifying a diplomatic relationship with any European power. While avoiding a costly war on the southern frontier was obviously the primary priority, the prospect of initiating a wholly new direction in American policy toward the Indians made the occasion even more significant. A treaty with the Creeks that recognized their legitimate claim to a large slice of land east of the Mississippi guaranteed by the federal government would serve as a model for all subsequent negotiations with the eastern tribes. Appearances were also important, because McGillivray, surely influenced by his extensive correspondence with British and Spanish allies, regarded the American republic as a highly problematic experiment destined to dissolve like all republics before it. From McGillivray's perspective, the centuries-old Creek Nation was sure to outlast this American upstart. Knox and Washington had planned the conspicuous display of political and military prowess in the national capital to show McGillivray that this republican experiment, unlike its European predecessors, was here to stay.[34]

The Creek delegation remained in New York for nearly a month. Most days were devoted to diplomatic negotiations, the evenings occupied by ceremonial celebrations that lubricated the daily sessions. There is some telltale evidence that McGillivray's evening lubrications left him with frequent hangovers the next day, but it is also possible that his periodic incapacitation was a result of his chronic ill-health.

One of the highlights on the ceremonial side was the viewing of a new portrait of Washington by John Trumbull, one of America's most prominent artists, who had also expressed a desire to paint a group portrait of the Creek chiefs, whose intrinsic nobility he compared to classical depictions of Roman senators. At the viewing of the Washington portrait, however, the Creeks shrieked with amazement and disbelief, because they had never before seen a picture that conveyed dimension on a flat surface. They accused Trumbull of practicing "magic" and refused to sit for him lest they fall victim to his spell.[35]

No record of the daily negotiations has survived, for the simple reason that no record was ever made. We do know that Knox assumed primary responsibility for the negotiations with McGillivray, and that he was joined by Thomas Jefferson, the recently arrived secretary of state, who brought his long-standing interest in Native American history and languages to the task. In his later career as president, Jefferson would oversee the process of gradual Indian removal that culminated in the Indian Removal Act (1830) under Andrew Jackson. But at this earlier stage of his career, Jefferson aligned himself squarely behind the Knox-Washington initiative to preserve Indian enclaves east of the Mississippi.[36]

One of his first acts as secretary of state was to draft a memorandum arguing that all the claims of the Yazoo companies were illegal, because Georgia had ceded all its western lands to the federal government upon joining the union. At Knox's request, he also drafted another legal opinion, arguing that the Creeks, like all Indian tribes, should be regarded as foreign nations. This in turn meant that all treaty provisions signed by the president and ratified by two-thirds of the Senate, including all trade provisions, immediately became the law of the land, and therefore invulnerable to legal challenge by any state or private company. Though he subsequently reversed himself on the latter score, regretting his endorsement of such unrestrained executive authority, at this moment Jefferson believed his highest duty as secretary of state was to support the policy of his president, and he marshaled the evidence to support the new-model treaty with the Creek Nation like a dedicated lawyer serving his client.[37]

At a deeper and less legislative level, moreover, Jefferson contributed the most fully articulated sense of the underlying moral issue at stake at this defining moment in the shaping of American policy toward the Native Americans. He had written the most compelling defense of Indian culture by any American of his time. In his *Notes on the State of Virginia,* Jefferson had devoted an entire section to "Aborigines," which attempted to recover the influence of Virginia's Indian tribes in shaping the history of the Old Dominion. More to the point, he had mounted a full-scale defense of Indian intelligence, courage, and integrity against the derogatory claims to the contrary by the eminent French scientist Count Buffon, who had argued that the American Indians were a biologically and mentally inferior collection of savages unworthy of comparison with white Europeans.[38]

Jefferson politely but firmly argued that Buffon, Europe's most renowned natural scientist, did not know what he was talking about. On the basis of personal observation and considerable study, Jefferson refuted each of Buffon's charges, offering dramatic evidence of Indian eloquence, physical bravery, and deeply ingrained sense of honor. All of which led to the conclusion that the Native Americans "are formed, in mind as well as in body, on the same model as Homo sapiens Europaeus." Whatever differences existed between Indians and Whites were a function of the primitive condition within which Indian culture currently found itself. (And Jefferson thought that, at least in some respects, Indian culture was actually superior; witness the number of white captives who preferred to live out their lives as Indians.) In the short term, this meant that no enlightened American or European could in good conscience dismiss Native Americans as savages in order to justify their dispersion and removal. And in the long term, it meant that the eventual assimilation of the Indian and Anglo-Saxon people of North America would benefit both races—a conclusion that Jefferson was unable to embrace with regard to the African Americans.[39]

Though it is likely that both Knox and Washington shared Jefferson's basic convictions about the integrity of Indian culture, neither of them had ever expressed himself so fully or so publicly on the issue. So Jefferson's addition to the diplomatic mix gave the unrecorded conversations of late July and early August 1790 a clearer moral foundation than they would otherwise have had. For different reasons, all three men had reached the same conclusion: Namely, the current negotiations with McGillivray and the Creeks offered the opportunity to place American Indian policy on a path that avoided the unjust and tragic fate toward which it was currently headed. And posterity would ultimately judge them on how they conducted themselves at this decisive moment.

McGillivray cared not a whit about posterity's judgment. His sole goal was to protect the Creek Nation from the demographic avalanche building to the east. His most pressing priority, then, was to block the claims of the Yazoo companies by enlisting federal support against the expansive pretensions of Georgia. He apparently extracted a personal promise from Knox that the United States government would do just that, for he later claimed that his major achievement during the negotiations was "to have signed the death sentence of the Company of the Yazoo."[40]

The core proposal in the American negotiating position was a federal guarantee, which in the end meant the deployment of troops, to maintain secure borders for the newly defined Creek Nation. But nothing in McGillivray's mentality permitted the fate of the Creeks to depend on trust in the word of any person or government. He saw himself engaged in a four-sided diplomatic game, simultaneously playing the United States government against the state of Georgia and the Americans against the Spanish. Any commitment he made to the Americans was temporary and conditional. It would expire if and when the American republic collapsed, which he thought to be imminent despite the conspicuous display of political permanence designed to impress him. Or it would be disowned whenever the Spanish made him a better offer. Or whichever came first.

What became known as the Treaty of New York passed the Senate on August 7, 1790, by a vote of fifteen to four. Both Georgia senators voted in the negative; one Georgia congressman, James Jackson, complained that the treaty gave away three million acres of Georgia's land to "a savage of the Creek nation," who had "been caressed in a most extraordinary manner, and sent home loaded with favors."[41]

The preamble to the treaty declared that it was designed to produce "peace and prosperity on our southern frontier" and to attach "the Creeks and the neighboring Tribes to the interests of the United States." In effect, the United States would displace Spain as the major ally and trading partner of the Creek Nation, which was now "under the protection of the United States of America and no other sovereign whatsoever." The eastern border of Creek Country was set at the Oconee River, about thirty miles west of McGillivray's preference on the Ogeechee, because so many white families had already settled in the disputed territory that removing them would be extremely difficult. The western border was left purposely ambiguous, allowing McGillivray to claim it was the Mississippi and the Americans to claim it did not stretch quite that far. A reasonable estimate of the new Indian protectorate would include modern-day western Georgia, southern Tennessee, northern Florida, all of Alabama, and eastern Mississippi. By any standard, it was a huge domain.[42]

Another provision implied, albeit discreetly, that the Creek

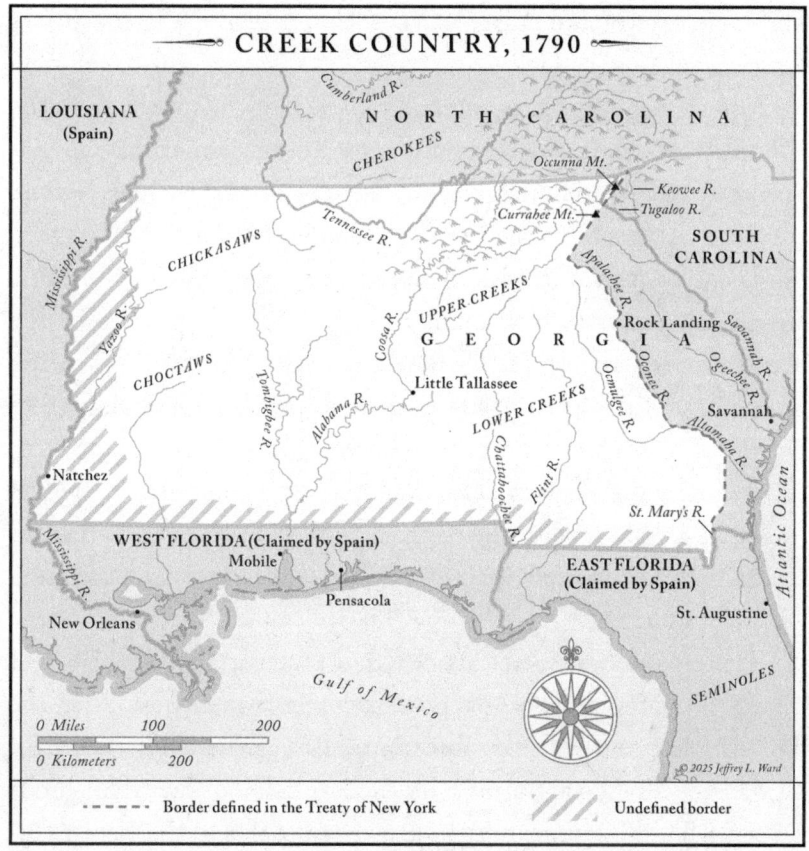

Map of Creek Country

homeland was supposed to shrink over time. "That the Creek Nation may be led to a greater degree of civilization," the treaty read, "and to become herdsmen and cultivators, instead of remaining in a state of hunters, the United States will from time to time furnish gratuitously the said nation with useful domestic animals and implements of husbandry." These apparently innocent words carried a hidden meaning that McGillivray surely recognized. The Creeks, who already practiced some farming, were being urged to make a complete transition to an agricultural economy, which would require much less land than a hunting-and-gathering economy. Left unsaid was that subsequent treaties would reduce the huge size of the current Creek Country. By how much was unspecified.[43]

Just as huge as the geographic area being defined as Creek Country was the promise being made by the American government: "The United States solemnly guarantee to the Creek Nation, all their lands within the limits of the United States to the westward and southward of the boundary described in the preceding article." No matter how ambiguous the current borders of the Creek Nation, and no matter how much they were likely to shrink in the future, the word of the national government was pledged to protect Creek Country from all encroachments by state governments and white settlers. This was a colossal commitment, which Knox regarded as politically essential for his entire enclave strategy, and economically preferable to a drawn-out series of Indian wars on the frontier.[44]

There were two secret articles, not included in the treaty but shared with the members of the Senate before their vote. First, the United States agreed to establish a trading partnership with their new Creek allies, starting at sixty thousand dollars' worth of goods a year. McGillivray insisted on a two-year delay in the implementation of this policy, putatively to work out the details of its operation, probably to use the time to see if he could get a better offer from the Spanish. Second, McGillivray was made a brigadier general in the American army, at an annual salary of twelve hundred dollars. Lesser Creek chiefs would receive lesser amounts. This obvious bribe was intended to replace the annual stipend McGillivray already received from the Spanish. Though such arrangements were too crassly corrupt to be mentioned in the treaty itself, McGillivray had made it known that he regarded them as common practice in all such negotiations and would be personally offended if the Americans failed to reward him for his service.[45]

The signing ceremony occurred August 13 at Federal Hall with the entire Congress in attendance. As befitted his new rank,

McGillivray wore a military uniform of blue faced with red. The other Creek chiefs, dressed in their most resplendent native costumes, entered the room shouting and shrieking words that one newspaper reporter described as eerily like war yells. The treaty was read aloud, and an interpreter provided a simultaneous translation for the Creeks. Washington then delivered a solemn address, pronouncing the Treaty of New York a mutually beneficial agreement between two great peoples. McGillivray responded in kind and thanked the people of New York for their gracious hospitality and Washington for his gift of beads and tobacco. All the chiefs then shook hands with Washington Indian-style, locking arms while grasping elbows. The Creeks then formed themselves into a chorus and sang a final song. The interpreter explained that it was about perpetual peace.[46]

○ ○ ○

Echoes of the Creek chorus had hardly died before the prospects for peace of any duration met the same fate. The unmanageable problem was demographic. Settlers on the Georgia frontier kept pouring across the newly established Creek borders by the thousands, blissfully oblivious to any geographic line drawn on the maps by some faraway government, cheered forward every step by the Georgia legislature, which saw them as foot soldiers in the Yazoo campaign for control of the southern frontier. Knox sent a detachment of federal troops to police the borders, but it was like stopping a flood with a bucket of sponges. Washington recognized the strategic dilemma right away. "Unless we can restrain the turbulence and disorderly conduct of our own borders," he observed, "it will be in vain to expect peace with the Indians—or that they will govern their own people better than we do ours." In his opinion, the white settlers and their promoters were the chief culprits, and it infuriated him that "a lawless set of unprincipled wretches . . .

can infringe the most solemn treaties, without receiving the punishment they so richly deserve." Washington eventually concluded
that "scarcely anything short of a Chinese wall will restrain the
Land jobbers and the encroachment of settlers upon the Indian
Country." He took the failure personally, believing that his signature on the Treaty of New York was his pledge of honor as well as
the solemn word of the United States government. Both were now
being exposed as worthless.[47]

Given the enormous issues at stake for the future of American
society, and given the truly tragic conclusion, there is an almost
irresistible urge to wonder if the story could have turned out differently. But if the tale told here is essentially correct, the answer must
be a dispiriting but firm no.

What stands out is the exceptional quality of leadership on
both sides of this defining moment. Knox and Washington, with
an assist from Jefferson, chose to defy the odds and transform
American policy toward the Native Americans. They did not do so
because it was politically expedient—quite the opposite. They did
so because the revolutionary fires still burned inside them and they
knew, deep down, that Indian removal was incompatible with the
republican values they cherished. They inherited an Indian policy
headed inexorably toward the extermination of Indian Country
east of the Mississippi, and they attempted to turn it around. Their
respective revolutionary credentials allowed them to argue, with
complete confidence, that principle needed to take precedence over
popular opinion. For, make no mistake, a referendum among the
white citizenry would have produced an overwhelming majority for
Indian removal. They made a heroic effort and they failed, though
it is difficult to imagine what they might have done differently to
change the outcome.

On the Indian side, it is also difficult to imagine a more capable
and shrewder leader than McGillivray. He played the cards that
were dealt him as deftly as possible. Though unscrupulous in the

realpolitik sense of the term, he was incorruptible whenever the fate of the Creek Nation was at stake, and his combination of pure intelligence, diplomatic agility, and sheer audacity made him the most effective Indian leader of his time. Looking back with all the advantages of hindsight, McGillivray remains the most impressive Indian leader we might have handpicked to avert the tragedy.

Why such failure amid such leadership? Part of the answer was sheer numbers. The white American population was doubling every twenty-five years at the same time the Indian population was declining at roughly the same rate. By the last decade of the eighteenth century, an ongoing demographic explosion was radiating out from the eastern rim of North America, and the Indian population opposing it was simply outnumbered and overwhelmed. No political effort to contain or control this explosion stood much chance of success.

Whatever chance did exist depended upon the capacity of the recently launched federal government to impose its will on the state of Georgia and the white population stretched across the southern frontier. In order to honor its promise of protection to the Creeks, the United States government needed to assume control over the eastern border of Creek Country, a roughly five-hundred-mile arc stretching from what is now eastern Tennessee to the Florida Panhandle. That in turn would have required a string of forts permanently garrisoned by at least ten thousand federal troops, this at a time when the entire American army was slightly more than one-third that size. At virtually every level—logistical, economic, political—there was not the remotest chance of implementing such a plan.[48]

Faced with the problem two hundred years later, the president would have nationalized the Georgia militia and ordered them to enforce the law defining the Creek borders, and the Supreme Court would have ruled that such actions were constitutional. None of these options were available to Washington, because the political institutions and legal precedents to make them possible were still aborning. In their absence, ultimate authority resided outside of government altogether, with those ordinary American citizens seeking a better life and a parcel of land to the west. In that sense, Indian removal was the inevitable consequence of unbridled democracy in action.

Part III

Southern Vistas

———◦—————

Nothing is more certainly written in the book of fate than that these people are to be free. Nor is it less certain that the two races, equally free, cannot live in the same government. Nature, habit, opinion have drawn indelible lines of distinction between them.

—THOMAS JEFFERSON, *Autobiography* (1824)

Chapter 8

Regrets at Mount Vernon

o o o

I had rather glide gently down the stream of life, leaving it
to posterity to think and say what they please of me.

—GEORGE WASHINGTON to James Craik, March 25, 1784

GEORGE WASHINGTON WAS an aficionado of exits. His two
most famous exits—in 1783, when he surrendered his commission at Annapolis, then in 1796, when he announced
his decision to retire from the presidency in his Farewell Address.
Though less famous, his third and final exit occurred in 1799, when
he drafted his will, his more personal farewell address, where he
declared his intention to liberate all the slaves he owned at Mount
Vernon.

"Upon the decease of my wife," he wrote, "it is my will and
desire that all the slaves I hold in my own right shall receive their
freedom." The young slaves should be supported until they reached
twenty-five years, taught to read and write, and "brought up to
some useful occupation." His final instruction concerned his long-
standing manservant Billy Lee, who had been hobbling about
Mount Vernon on two badly damaged knees for several years. Billy
should be freed outright upon Washington's death and provided
with a small annuity along with room and board, "as a testimony to

my sense of his attachment to me, and for his faithful service during the Revolutionary War."[*][1]

Washington also stipulated that his freed slaves must be permitted to reside in Virginia. The standard practice for most Virginia planters who freed their slaves was to require that they be sent elsewhere, least they contaminate the Anglo-Saxon bloodlines of the white population, a policy endorsed by Thomas Jefferson and passed into law by the Virginia legislature a few years after Washington's death. Within the prominent members of Virginia's planter class, Washington was a singular figure, not just for freeing his slaves, but for holding open the prospect of an emerging biracial society in the Old Dominion. A majority of the slaves freed at Mount Vernon settled in Fairfax County in a community they named Freetown, where several of their descendants continue to reside.[2]

○ ○ ○

Washington's will was the culmination of a long and somewhat tortured process that had its origins in the postwar years, more specifically in December 1785, when he received an unsolicited letter from a plantation owner named Robert Pleasants. The Virginia legislature had recently enacted a law permitting slaveowners to free their slaves without seeking approval from the state government, and Pleasants, a Quaker, had accordingly emancipated all eighty of his own slaves on Virginia's Eastern Shore. Pleasants

---

* Washington owned slightly fewer than half the 317 slaves at Mount Vernon when he died in December 1799, only five months after completing his will. Martha owned the remainder, called "dower slaves," whom she inherited upon her first husband's death. There is strong evidence that Martha did not share Washington's antislavery convictions, but she did honor the terms of his will. When the slaves at Mount Vernon learned that their emancipation was contingent upon Martha's death, rumors circulated that they planned to poison her. She promptly freed them in January 1801.

wanted to know why Washington had not done the same thing. "How strange it must appear to impartial thinking men," Pleasants lectured, "to be informed that many who were warm advocates of the noble cause during the war are now sitting down in a state of ease, dissipation, and extravagance on the labor of slaves."

Pleasants ended with an argument almost designed to catch Washington's attention. "For not withstanding Thou art now receiving a tribute of praise from a grateful people," he warned, "the time is coming when all actions shall be weighed in an equal balance. How sad it would then be," Pleasants concluded, "to learn that the great hero of American independence had failed the final test by holding a number of people in absolute slavery, who by nature are equally entitled to freedom as himself." By failing to free his slaves at Mount Vernon, in effect, Washington was placing his legacy on the wrong side of American history, where it was eventually destined to languish in obscurity.[3]

At the same time that Pleasants was drafting his letter, Washington was hosting a steady flow of artists at Mount Vernon. "I am now so hackneyed to the touches of the Painter's pencil," he confessed, "that I am altogether at their behest and sit like Patience on a Monument whilst they are delineating the lines of my face." The Pleasants letter arrived during the visit of Jean-Antoine Houdon, France's most distinguished sculptor, who had traveled all the way from Paris to make a life mask for his projected statue of Washington. Washington complained to Lafayette that the tedious sessions with Houdon were like mandatory military formations that must be tolerated, because artists like Houdon were "the doorkeepers of the temple of fame," who "held the keys of the gate by which Patriots, Sages, and Heroes were admitted to immortality."[4]

Based on earlier letters to Lafayette, we know that Washington no longer believed in the Christian version of immortality in heaven (or hell). When he died, he was only going to "the dreary mansions of my fathers," which meant into the ground. Which in turn meant that the only credible version of immortality that Washington regarded as realistic was to live on in the memory of future generations. There was no heaven, only posterity. Houdon and those intrusive painters were temporary annoyances, to be sure, but also invaluable accomplices in making him an immortal icon in the only way that really mattered. According to Pleasants, however, failure to free his slaves at Mount Vernon would cast a dark shadow across his legacy, and therefore his place in the American pantheon.[5]

Washington struggled with this issue for the remaining years of his life. As noticed earlier, he had felt no twinges of guilt at demanding the return of his escaped slaves after Yorktown, then again during the British evacuation of New York. But he later refused to endorse or assist efforts by other Virginia slaveowners to recover their runaways, not wishing his name associated with a recovery project that would not play well with posterity.

There is some evidence, admittedly controversial, that he was considering a plan to emancipate his slaves prior to his inauguration as president, thereby making a public statement of enduring significance for all future occupants of the office. Here are the words that Washington allegedly spoke on the eve of his inauguration, as recorded by David Humphreys, his former aide and future biographer:

> The unfortunate condition of the persons, whose labour in part I employed, has been the unavoidable subject of regret. To make the Adults among them as easy and comfortable in their circumstances as their actual state of ignorance and improvidence would admit and to lay a foundation to prepare the rising generation for a destiny different from that in which they were born, afforded some satisfaction to my mind, and could not I hoped be displeasing to the Creator.[6]

The historian Henry Wiencek has speculated that Washington decided to use his looming presidency as the occasion to emancipate his legacy from the Mount Vernon burden, and thereby establish a political precedent for the office of president that would echo through the ages. My own best guess is that the quotation is more Humphreys than Washington. The Humphreys biography appeared after Washington's death, and Humphreys, so I suggest, transposed Washington's language in his will from 1799 to 1789. Nothing in the public record supports the claim that Washington was considering the course of action that Humphreys claimed.

A surprisingly large portion of Washington's letters during his presidency concerned Mount Vernon. (One gets a clear sense that he would have much preferred to be there than New York or Philadelphia. Indeed, no president in American history did not want to be president more than George Washington.) Most of his letters focused on where to plant trees, dig trenches, or construct fences, but another refrain runs through the correspondence. As he put it, "how to get quit of Negroes." He confessed to a friend, "I do not like to think, much less talk about it." But he could not stop worrying about it, for, as much as any decision he had made as General Washington during the war, this decision would determine his place in the history books.[7]

Three entrenched obstacles blocked his path forward.

First, the slaves he owned and the dower slaves owned by Martha had intermarried over the years, and Washington had vowed never to split up families. Unless he renounced that vow, no scheme for emancipation was feasible, and if he did so, he risked limiting Martha's control of the dower slaves, whom she intended to pass on to her grandchildren.

Second, Washington faced a financial problem if and when he managed to free his slaves, which he felt compelled to resolve beforehand. In order to sustain the comfortable lifestyle that he and Martha had enjoyed at Mount Vernon, what he called "tranquility with a certain income," Washington needed to generate a fresh flow of cash. In May 1794, he announced his decision to sell off a portion of the huge tract of land on the Great Kanawha River and in the Ohio County that—the ironies abound—the British government had bestowed for his services in the French and Indian War. He wanted his intentions for selling his western lands kept secret, lest they expose his plan, as he put it, "to liberate a certain species of property which I possess, very repugnantly to my own feelings."[8]

The problem with Washington's plan was that the moral outcome, emancipation, was held hostage to the notoriously capricious land market in the western territories, which never managed to meet Washington's somewhat inflated valuation of his property. As a result, two years into his retirement he found himself in much the same predicament he had faced at the start: Mount Vernon's expanding slave population—he counted 317 in 1799—only a minority of whom could be gainfully employed; ownership of vast tracts in the west that he valued at over five hundred thousand dollars,* but that no one wished to purchase at a price he deemed fair; annual costs at Mount Vernon that were outrunning his income; and the moral shadow of slavery still hanging over his head and his legacy.

A third obstacle, neither legal nor financial, blocked his path toward the destination that he knew in his soul would assure his own destiny. But the obstacle was in fact his own soul, which had taken shape in his youth—he had owned his first slave when he was eleven years old, and prior to the war had become a prominent Virginia squire with a plantation, an enslaved workforce, and all the material comforts of a privileged and dominating lifestyle. Although his experience during the war had exposed Washing-

---

* In current currency, Washington was a multimillionaire.

ton to a larger world of egalitarian values, it was built on a more presumptive and primal set of assumptions that never went away. Just as his own slaves and the dower slaves were entangled on his plantation, his desire to free his slaves was entangled in the roots of his own origins as the master of Mount Vernon, whose control over others was unquestioned—indeed, the centerpiece of his dominating personality.

Washington's old self was put on display during the early years of his retirement, when he attempted to recover Ona Judge, who had fled the presidential mansion in May 1796 and eventually settled in New Hampshire as a free woman. Described as "a light mulatto girl, about twenty years old, much freckled, slender and delicately formed," Judge was Martha's personal maid, previously valued for her loyalty and wide-ranging competence. Martha made it clear to Washington that every effort should be made to get her back.[9]

When, after several attempts, Washington made contact with Judge, she expressed a willingness to return and "serve with fidelity," on the condition that she be freed upon the death of both Washington and Martha. These were precisely the terms that Washington was considering for his will, though because she was a dower slave, he lacked the legal authority to free her. He might have explained his dilemma to Judge, encouraged her understandable urge for freedom, then wished her well, but that is not what he did. Here are the words of his response:

To enter into such a compromise with her is totally inadmissible, for reasons that must strike at first view. For however well-disposed I might be to a gradual abolition, or even to an entire emancipation of that description of People, it would neither be politic or just to reward with premature preference, and thereby [generate] discontent in the minds of her fellow servants, who by their steady attachments are far more deserving than herself of favor.[10]

Washington was incapable of regarding Judge as an equal partner in a dialogue about her own fate. At his very core, he continued to harbor the long-standing assumptions of a Virginia slaveowner: Judge was a piece of property that he owned, not a self-possessed young woman with a mind of her own. What Washington apparently found so offensive was that, once free, Judge refused to behave like a slave. She exposed that Washington, despite his evolution toward the promised land of emancipation as a public figure, continued to think like a typical Virginia slaveowner in his private role as master of Mount Vernon. Beyond and beneath the legal and financial roadblocks to doing what was clearly the right thing for his legacy in his will, there was a layer of emotional resistance rooted in his role as lord and master of his Mount Vernon kingdom. It was hard for Washington to surrender that status. This was the major reason he kept delaying the decision, and the decisive reason why he relegated it to his will, to take effect only after he was dead and gone.

o o o

Given the significance of the slavery issue, there is one section of Washington's will that scholars have understandably tended to ignore—namely, the apportionment of his other property. The customary practice within wealthy families was an unequal distribution, which preserved the core of the estate in one branch of the family in order to assure the continuation of a dynasty that would live on under the patriarch's name well into the future. Washington opted for an equal division among multiple heirs in order to assure that, as an ancestral presence, he would disappear.

Although Jefferson wrote lyrical tributes to the idea that "the earth belongs to the living," it was Washington who put the principle into practice.[11]

His decision to divide Mount Vernon into five separate plots with different heirs embodied the same distributive principle and the same preferred outcome. He wanted Mount Vernon itself to disappear. It was the centerpiece of his life, but he did not want it to become the centerpiece of his legacy, for the obvious reason that it would focus the attention of posterity on his role as a slaveowner.

Mount Vernon was well on its way to the oblivion Washington wanted when a small group of predominantly southern women, calling itself the Mount Vernon Ladies' Association, purchased the estate just before the start of the Civil War. It was only the beginning of a long recovery process that, in fact, continues to the present day, and that, especially over the last half-century, has focused on literally digging up the history of the African American occupants of the plantation. Many of the roughly one million tourists a year tend to regard Mansion House and Washington's immediate family as their primary interest, but the full tour carries all comers into the world of the enslaved workforce, the fields where they worked, the dwellings where they lived, and the graveyards where they are buried.[12]

Any attempt to assess Washington's place in the American pantheon without focusing on his life at Mount Vernon is both futile and misguided, even though Washington himself apparently wished us to do precisely that. The Washington Monument more accurately captures his preferred kind of memorial, the largest structure on the Mall or Tidal Basin, and the only one with no words: a monument to a monument.

Mount Vernon, on the other hand, is a tribute to a man and to the enslaved workforce that he described as both his family and his property. It therefore inherently focuses attention on the great contradiction of the founding era, that America's greatest leader during that era, who did more than any prominent Virginia slave-holder to resolve the slavery dilemma, ultimately acknowledged that it was "the only unavoidable subject of [my] regret." This was the legacy he most wished to obscure. And, for that very reason, the legacy we most need to comprehend.*

---

* During his first term as president, Washington apprised his Cabinet that, if the current sectional split should become a civil war during his lifetime, he would side with the north. Thomas Jefferson leaked the revelation to his Virginia friends, who from that time forward regarded Mount Vernon as an enemy outpost.

Chapter 9

Memories at Monticello

o o o

The sentiment of Thomas Jefferson was very fine in theory,
but would have been enhanced a thousand fold if Jefferson
practiced what he preached. Precept without example is like
faith without works—it [is] dead.

— JOHN LANGTON to Benjamin Franklin, May 6, 1788

THE DYING LEAVES WERE falling to the ground on the
slopes of Monticello in the late fall of 1824. Riding up the
eastern slope of the mountain was the Marquis de Lafayette, accompanied by an escort of 120 mounted men and a crowd
of two hundred local dignitaries and curious onlookers, eager to
witness the reunion of two relics from the preceding generation.
Like the leaves, Lafayette and Thomas Jefferson were making a
final appearance. As the two aging patriots tottered toward each
other and embraced, several witnesses claimed they saw two ghosts
from a bygone era.[1]

As it turned out, the real ghost at the reunion was already as
dead as the falling leaves. Neither Jefferson nor Lafayette wished to
acknowledge it, but any hope for ending slavery, or placing the great
contradiction of the American founding on the road to extinction,
had come and gone. They could never have imagined that outcome

in their earlier incarnation as revolutionaries a half-century earlier, when the political momentum of what they called "The Cause" seemed poised to sweep slavery into the oblivion it deserved.

Facing that failure was not going to be easy, especially given Jefferson's insistence that any robust form of argument violated the unspoken code of conduct on his mountaintop. But avoiding it was going to be difficult, since Lafayette had alerted Jefferson that he was coming with a personal reprimand of his old friend for abandoning his previous leadership role in the campaign to abolish slavery. "I would like before I die," he had warned, "to be assured that progressive and earnest measures have been adopted to attain in due time so desirable, so necessary an object."[2]

Moreover, Lafayette also carried with him an address from the free black community of Boston, recently published in the *Columbian Centinel* and reprinted in several northern newspapers, which posed the very question that Lafayette wanted Jefferson to answer.

> *As the Whites gained the Freedom for which they contended,*
> *Could you have supposed, when the war had thus ended,*
> *That they would hand over the African race,*
> *To Thraldom unceasing, and endless disgrace—*
> *Inflicting more evils, as thousands to one,*
> *Than the Rulers of Britain on them had e're done?*[*][3]

o o o

Jefferson had been practicing an answer to that question for more than thirty years. His earliest defense of his conduct was perhaps designed to be disarming—namely, that he had not abandoned the

---

* The one woman in Lafayette's entourage, Frances "Fanny" Wright, brought credentials as a prominent British writer, and was also an outspoken abolitionist with a reputation for unladylike candor. Fanny was Lafayette's secret weapon to penetrate Jefferson's vaunted network of defenses on the slavery issue.

core values of The Cause but, rather, that they had abandoned him. At the high altitude where Jefferson did his best thinking, emancipation was supposed to be self-enacting, meaning that slavery would die a natural death because it was a vestige of the Dark Ages, like a belief in miracles and witchcraft. It was also an economic anachronism, incompatible with free labor, an idea he probably borrowed from Adam Smith. He had done his best as a young man to articulate the revolutionary principles, most resoundingly in the Declaration of Independence, but somehow the anachronism of slavery had not died. It was now the mission of the next generation to carry on the work that he and his generation had begun. In the meantime, his highest obligation was to care for his own slaves at Monticello as a benevolent patriarch and wait for history to unfold along the lines he had envisioned. Leadership meant waiting.

Lafayette had taken a different path. (That his path somehow avoided the guillotine in Paris had all the markings of a miracle.) As early as 1783, soon after the war for independence had been won, Lafayette approached George Washington with a proposal to free all his slaves at Mount Vernon, then employ them as tenants in a model community in what eventually became West Virginia, arguing, "Such an Example of Yours Might Render it a General Practice." Lafayette himself had used his considerable fortune to purchase the island of Cayenne, off the coast of French Guiana, there to establish a school designed to prepare freed slaves for freedom. (The French government eventually assumed control over Cayenne and made it the notorious prison camp called Devil's Island.) He called Cayenne "my Hobby Horse," meaning his lifelong project to facilitate the transition from slavery to eventual assimilation as free men and women. In effect, Lafayette had always believed that enslaved Blacks could and should become equal members of American society. At roughly the same time that Lafayette was reaching that conclusion, however, Jefferson was reaching a quite different one.[4]

His position on slavery had hardened into a bimodal pattern during the mid-1780s. On one side of his mind, slavery was, as he put it in *Notes on the State of Virginia* (1785), "a perpetual exercise of the most boisterous passions, the most unremitting despotisms on the one part, and degrading submissions on the other. Indeed, I tremble for my country when I reflect that God is just." No American statesman in the founding era put it more ardently or defiantly.

But the other side of his mind spoke with equivalent passion against the creation of a biracial American society. "The opinion that they are inferior in the faculties of reason and imagination must be regarded with diffidence," he observed in *Notes*. Still, his conclusion was anything but diffident: "Blacks are inferior to whites in the endowments of both mind and body." Any mixing of the two races would, therefore, generate an inferior American race, so "when freed they must be removed beyond the reach of mixture."[5]

He had summed up his double-edged message most succinctly in his unpublished autobiography (1821): "Nothing is more certainly written in the book of fate than that these people are to be set free. Nor is it less certain that the two races, equally free, cannot live in the same government. Nature, habit, opinion have drawn indelible lines of distinction between them." It therefore followed that no plan for emancipation could go forward until arrangements to transport the entire freed black population beyond America's borders was implemented. Until that happened, any and all discussions of emancipation were ludicrous. Ending slavery was thereby held hostage to what Jefferson called "expatriation." It was a recipe for self-imposed paralysis.[6]

Only a few months before Lafayette's visit, Jefferson had made his most exhaustive effort to calculate the cost of deporting all the freed slaves. He concluded that the price tag for removing one and a half million ex-slaves over a twenty-five-year period would be nine hundred million dollars—several trillion dollars in modern currency. Once you looked at that number, he realized, it would be "impossible to look at this question a second time." Not only that, but during the twenty-five years when the removal plan would be working, the size of the enslaved population would double, creating an endless effort to reverse the centuries-old African diaspora. His rationale for waiting until a removal plan was in place effectively collapsed, since the waiting period would last forever.[7]

Jefferson felt no obligation to share this depressing insight with Lafayette and his entourage; in fact, his subsequent silence on the issue suggests he failed to share it with himself. Throughout Lafayette's ten-day visit, Jefferson kept him busy touring the campus of his proudest creation, the University of Virginia, where his architectural centerpiece, the Rotunda, was conveniently being dedicated. The only way that the topic of slavery could come up was if Lafayette insisted, and Jefferson saw to it that his guests were kept too busy admiring the architecture of the Rotunda and the ongoing improvements of his mansion-on-the-mountain. It also helped that Jefferson was a genius at avoiding any subject that roamed too far from his elevated and often visionary comfort zone, where all the eternal truths were self-evident.

But architecture, albeit of a different sort, posed an unavoidable and awkward problem. When historians talk about the architecture of Monticello, they are almost always referring to the Palladian style that Jefferson had come to love during his travels in southern France, then used as the design for his mansion. But the architecture of Monticello as a plantation was of a different genre altogether, structured to make the black workforce up and down the mountain almost invisible, and to feature the light-skinned household slaves, who looked and acted like members of the family because, in fact, many of them were. An earlier French visitor described the scene: "In Virginia mongrel negros are found in greater numbers than in Carolina and Georgia; and I have seen, especially at Mr. Jefferson's home, slaves who neither in point of colour or features showed the least trace of their original descent from Africa; but their mothers being slaves, they retain the same condition."[8]

The ironies abound, since the core appeal of the biracial façade at Monticello was the up-front slaves, whose privileged status and domestic demeanor seemed to defy the coercive conditions and darker skin color customarily associated with the institution of slavery. And yet this biracial version of Jefferson's workforce was also a palpable advertisement of precisely the kind of racial mixing that Jefferson claimed to abhor, and used to justify his prevailing paralysis.

How Lafayette and his young secretary, Auguste Levasseur, processed the scene during mealtimes at Monticello never made it into the historical record. But the scene invites, almost compels, serious speculation. Did they wonder which of the mostly white servants were Jefferson's children? If so, did they try to read Jefferson's face for traces of affection? Or perhaps for signs of forced disinterest? What did they say to each other once back in their rooms? That Jefferson's composure derived from his long experience of living a blatant contradiction? Or was he, even more blatantly, living a lie? Was there any French thinker or school of thought capable of explaining the mental or emotional denial mechanism necessary to sustain sanity, even serenity, while enjoying the benefits of a barbaric institution he seriously claimed to abhor? Or was Jefferson's long-stated aversion to racial mixing rooted in his personal experience with its deepest physical and sexual attractions?

Such questions were all taboo on Jefferson's mountaintop, but Levasseur did covertly place slavery in the historical record with his observations about the relative backwardness of Virginia society, especially when contrasted with bustling towns and villages that he and Lafayette had visited in the northern states. The Old Dominion had in fact become a cultural wasteland of sleepy towns, impassable roads, depleted soil, and slovenly citizenry, whose major occupation was not to have one. The source of all this visible decrepitude and decline was quite obvious, so self-evident that it need not be mentioned. It was almost as if the residents of Virginia, the former fountainhead of political leadership during the glory days that both Lafayette and Jefferson could remember so fondly, had consciously decided to surrender their state's previous primacy and, almost intentionally, allowed it to become irrelevant.[9]

Coincidentally, shortly after Lafayette's visit, Jefferson received a letter from his granddaughter Ellen Randolph Coolidge that made the same point. Coolidge had married into a prominent Boston family, and the trips she and her husband took through the towns and villages that dotted the New England countryside had a major impact on her inherited southern sensibilities. "It has given me an idea of prosperity and improvement," she wrote, "such as I fear the Southern States cannot hope for as long as the cancer of slavery eats into their hearts, and diseases the whole body by the ulcer at the core."[10]

In his response, Jefferson acknowledged that slavery was "our fatal stain, that deforms what Nature has bestowed on us of her fairest gifts." But decisive action to end slavery could only occur once the freed slaves were transported elsewhere. Otherwise, the "fatal stain" of blackness would "forever darken and forever contaminate what Nature has bestowed on us." He did not mention that his recent calculations had revealed that no plan for black removal was logistically or financially feasible. Best not to burden his grandchildren with insoluble dilemmas.[11]

ο ο ο

Lafayette and Levasseur stopped at Monticello for a brief and final visit in August 1825, on their way back to New York and then Paris. But Jefferson was indisposed, perhaps with the early symptoms of the intestinal cancer that would end his life eleven months later. Not that any conclusive conversations could have occurred if Jefferson had somehow rallied one last time. It was already clear that the two veterans of the American Revolution agreed about the historic significance of American independence, but disagreed about the viability of a biracial American society.

More personally, they disagreed about the meaning of Jefferson's magic words in the Declaration of Independence. For Lafayette, the words were truly magic, meaning that all human beings, regardless of race or gender, possessed natural rights that no society could either restrict or deny. For Jefferson, "men" meant white males, with perhaps a vague hope that white women might be included in some distant future.

All Blacks, men and women, occupied a lower and inferior stratum of the human race. Lafayette believed in the most expansive understanding of the Jeffersonian promise. Jefferson himself did not.

∘ ∘ ∘

Although it apparently never occurred to Jefferson, one of the arguments he could have made when asked why he did not free his slaves was that he no longer owned them; his creditors did. During his retirement years, Jefferson's debt kept growing, eventually reaching more than a hundred thousand dollars, the modern equivalent of millions. (Almost the entire planter class in Virginia claimed that the principle of compound interest defied their comprehension.) But eventually the depth of his indebtedness defied even Jefferson's awesome powers of denial, and the looming probability of his own death quashed the long-standing illusion that something would turn up before he headed for the hereafter.

He confided to James Monroe that he was never very good at keeping an account book, so "the real wonder is that I should have been so long as sixty years in reaching the result to which I am now reduced." The inimitable Jefferson style rescued him from total despair. "A call on me to the amount of my endorsement," he wrote Madison, "would indeed close my course by a catastrophe I had never calculated." Both Madison and Monroe would also die bankrupt, victims of an inherently unprofitable slave economy that none of them could find a way to end without releasing the emancipated slaves into the purportedly pure white population.[12]

Jefferson mustered a final surge of eloquence in response to a request for his thoughts on the fiftieth anniversary of the Declaration of Independence. "All eyes are opened or opening to the rights of man," he wrote. "The general spread of the light of science has already laid open to every view the palpable truth that the mass of mankind has not been born with saddles on their backs, nor a favored few, booted and spurred, ready to ride them legitimately, by the grace of God."[13]

If those inspiring words were still floating in the air at Monticello during the public auction six months later, no one heard them. Least of all the "130 valuable Negros" who were sold to the highest bidder, a fate that Jefferson had vowed would never happen. It was a tragedy for all concerned. Slave families were broken up and dispersed throughout Virginia and "down the river" to the brutal cotton fields of Mississippi and Louisiana. Jefferson's surviving daughter and her eleven children were made wards of the state, dependent upon charitable contributions from state governments. (Virginia could not offer assistance because its economy, like Monticello's, was bankrupted by slavery. Indeed, its only cash crop was its surplus slaves.) Jefferson was under the ground, shielded once again—this time forever—from the inevitable implications of his beguiling delusions.

o o o

But the ghost of Jefferson continued to hover over the debate in Virginia about the future of slavery in the Old Dominion. The debate reached a crescendo in 1831, when the Virginia legislature met in a special session to confront the question frontally: Should Virginia follow the northern states and commit to a gradual emancipation plan? Or follow the states of the deep south in the other direction? Advocates of the former option envisioned Virginia abandoning tobacco as a cash crop in favor of wheat and corn, in effect becoming a southern extension of Pennsylvania. There were obvious economic advantages to that option, as all the bankrupt planters in Tidewater could testify. But there were also racial implications that, so it turned out, were more politically potent.

A county-by-county referendum revealed that an overwhelming majority of the white population in Virginia objected to any plan for ending slavery that did not include a provision for removing the freed slaves from the state. Until such a removal plan was adopted, all talk of emancipation was premature.[14]

A professor at the College of William and Mary, Thomas Dew, took the next step. In *Review of the Debate in the Virginia Legislatures,* Dew argued that all talk of ending slavery should not just be postponed, it should be ended, because no less a source than Thomas Jefferson had concluded that no removal plan was financially or politically possible. Dew's pamphlet was widely circulated throughout the southern states, where it was regarded as Virginia's declaration of dependence on slavery, in effect a clarification of Jefferson's magic words to mean "all white men are created equal."[15]

Virginia was consciously choosing to continue its downward spiral as an economic and cultural backwater, where the planter class, like Jefferson, would die bankrupt, where the white working class refused to work, with the uplifting idea of a Virginia Dynasty just a bygone memory. Looking forward, one could safely predict that prominent leaders in Virginia would wrap themselves in the Confederate flag, embrace the myth of the "Lost Cause," vehemently oppose the civil rights movement, and derive their sense of significance by standing proudly on the wrong side of American history.

As for Jefferson, he will forever be remembered for his iconic eloquence in the Declaration of Independence, but his failure to live up to his own words ended in tragedy for him, his black and white families, and decades of decline for the Commonwealth he so loved.[16]

Acknowledgments

At a certain age, one looks back to the beginning and realizes that a few teachers put you on the path you have traveled. Five historians were my guides: Winthrop Jordan at William and Mary; C. Vann Woodward, Elting Morison, and Edmund Morgan at Yale; and William McFeely at Mount Holyoke. Although they are all gone, their voices are still alive in me.

Five friends read the entire manuscript and let me know what they liked and what could be improved: Victor Hennigsen, Robert Moore, Mary Mulligan, Stacy Schiff, and Steve Smith. The book is dedicated to Steve, a master of that sacred space where substance meets style, who has been editing my prose for over thirty years.

My old roommate at Yale, Gad Heuman, guided me through the extensive British scholarship on the slave trade. Louise Harlow, a former actress and current archivist, sent me several out-of-print books on the Laurens family and slavery in South Carolina. Louise was also a cheerleader from beginning to end, whom I kept trying not to disappoint. The editorial staff of the *Washington Papers* never put me on hold.

The book was written in longhand with a five-point rollerball pen in my study atop Hawk Mountain in central Vermont. I cannot manage research assistants, but my personal assistant for over thirty years, Linda Chesky Fernandes, managed just about everything else, which included deciphering my scrawl and compensating for my technological incompetence. Two very large Labradoodles, Lucy and Desi, slept beside me as I scribbled, and instinctively knew when to take me for a walk. My wife, Ellen Wilkins Ellis, did not edit my writing, but did edit my psyche. I have a hunch that made a huge difference.

My agent, Bob Barnett, negotiated the contract at Knopf with a minimum of fuss, and checked in periodically to ask how it was going. My editor at Knopf, Victoria Wilson, lived up to her reputation as an ardent advocate for her authors within the house.

Finally, I should acknowledge that the entire book was written during a deeply divided political climate in which it was impossible to ignore the persistent potency of the thinly disguised racial prejudice inherent in the slogan to "Make America Great Again." We are currently living through a backlash pattern that, at least as I see it, had its origins during the American founding.

Notes

The notes below represent my attempt to provide documentation for all the quotations in the text, the vast majority of which come from primary sources. When the story I try to tell crosses over contested historical terrain, I have cited secondary sources that strike me as seminal. My accounting on that score, however, is far from exhaustive, because such a standard would burden the book with notes that outweigh the text.

I have modernized spelling and punctuation, except when the eighteenth-century version is not confusing and adds a distinctive flavor the reader might find revealing. I have capitalized both Black and White when used as nouns, lowercased both when used as adjectives.

Three chapters draw heavily upon research published in previous books: chapter five upon chapters four, five, and six in *The Quartet;* chapter six upon chapter three in *Founding Brothers;* chapter seven upon chapter four in *American Creation.*

Abbreviations

Am Ar Peter Force, ed., *American Archives,* 9 vols. (Washington, D.C., 1833–53).

AFC Lynn Butterfield et al., eds., *Adams Family Correspondence,* 13 vols. to date (Cambridge, Mass., 1963–).

AIUS Wilcomb Washburn, ed., *The American Indian and the United States: A Documentary History,* 4 vols. (New York, 1973).

AP Robert Taylor, et al., eds., *The Papers of John Adams,* 17 vols. to date (Cambridge, Mass., 1983–).

DA Lyman H. Butterfield, ed., *The Diary and Autobiography of John Adams,* 4 vols. (Cambridge, Mass., 1966).

DHRC Merrill Jensen, John Kaminski, and Gaspar Saladino, eds., *Documentary History of the Ratification of the Constitution*, 26 vols. (Madison, Wisc., 1976–).

JCC W. C. Ford et al., eds., *Journals of the Jefferson Continental Congress*, 24 vols. (Washington, D.C., 1904–37).

JP Julian Boyd et al., eds., *The Papers of Thomas Jefferson*, 32 vols. to date (Princeton, N.J., 1950–).

JJP Elizabeth M. Nuxall et al., eds., *The Papers of John Jay* (Charlottesville, Va., 2010–).

LDC Paul H. Smit et al., eds., *Letters of Delegates to Congress, 1774–1789*, 29 vols. (Washington, D.C., 1976–2000).

LP David R. Chestnut and C. James Taylor, eds., *The Papers of Henry Laurens*, 17 vols. (Columbia, S.C., 1968–2003).

MP William T. Hutchinson et al., eds., *The Papers of James Madison*, 15 vols. (Chicago and Charlottesville, Va., 1962–).

PAR Gordon S. Wood, *The American Revolution: Writings from the Pamphlet Debate, 1764–1776*, 2 vols., *Library of America* (New York, 2011).

PWCS W. W. Abbot and Dorothy Twohig, eds., *The Papers of George Washington: The Confederation Series*, 6 vols. (Charlottesville, Va., 1992–97).

PWPS W. W. Abbot and Dorothy Twohig, eds., *The Papers of George Washington: Presidential Series*, 22 vols. to date (Charlottesville, Va., 1981–).

PWRS W. W. Abbot, Dorothy Twohig, and Alexander Chase, eds., *The Papers of George Washington: Revolutionary War Series*, 22 vols. to date (Charlottesville, Va., 1985–).

PWRT W. W. Abbot, ed., *The Papers of George Washington: Retirement Series*, 4 vols. (Charlottesville, Va., 1988–89).

RL James Morton Smith, ed., *The Republic of Letters: The Correspondence Between Thomas Jefferson and James Madison*, 3 vols. (New York, 2017).

WAR Clifford R. Rogers, Ty Seidule, and Samuel J. Watson, eds., *The West Point History of the American Revolution* (New York, 2017).

WMQ *William and Mary Quarterly*, 3rd series.

WW James C. Fitzpatrick, ed., *Writings of George Washington*, 39 vols. (Washington, D.C., 1931–39).

Persons

AA   Abigail Adams
AH   Alexander Hamilton
GW   George Washington
HL   Henry Laurens
JA   John Adams
JJ   John Jay
JM   James Madison
TJ   Thomas Jefferson

Chapter 1
AN AMERICAN DILEMMA

1. Quoted in Hugh Thomas, *The Slave Trade: The Story of the Atlantic Slave Trade, 1440–1870* (New York, 1997), 302.

2. David Hackett Fischer, *African Founders: How Enslaved People Expanded American Ideals* (New York, 2022), 117–18; Francis Moore, *Travels into the Inland Parts of Africa* (London, 1738), 42; Trevor Burnard, "The Atlantic Slave Trade," in Gad Heuman and Trevor Burnard, eds., *The Routledge History of Slavery* (London, 2012), 80–98.

3. David Eltis and David Richardson, *Atlas of the Transatlantic Slave Trade* (New Haven, 2010). Older but still valuable is Philip D. Curtin, *The Atlantic Slave Trade: A Census* (Madison, Wisc., 1969). For the trade from the Caribbean to North America, see Gregory E. O'Malley, *Final Passages: The Intercolonial Slave Trade of British America, 1619–1807* (Chapel Hill, N.C., 2014), 2–29.

4. Fischer, *African Founders*, 1–31.

5. Evarts B. Greene and Virginia D. Harrington, *American Population Before the Federal Census of 1790* (New York, 1932), 136–38.

6. Winthrop D. Jordan, *White over Black: American Attitudes Toward the Negro, 1550–1812* (Chapel Hill, N.C., 1968), 212–15, 271–75; Thomas, *Slave Trade*, 465–78; David Brion Davis, *The Problem of Slavery in the Age of Revolution, 1770–1823* (New York, 1999), 286–99.

7. George Whitefield, *Three Letters from the Reverend Mr. G. Whitefield* (Philadelphia, 1740), 15; John Woolman, *Considerations on Keeping Negroes* (Philadelphia, 1762), 353–68.

8. Jean R. Soderlund, *Quakers and Slavery: A Divided Spirit* (Princeton, 1985); Maurice Jackson, *Let This Voice Be Heard: Anthony Benezet, Father of Atlantic Abolitionism* (Philadelphia, 2009); Anthony Benezet, *A Short Account of That Part of Africa Inhabited by the Negroes* (Philadelphia, 1762), and *Observations on the Enslaving, Importing and Purchasing of Negroes* (Germantown, Pa., 1760).

9. Thomas, *Slave Trade*, 273; Greene and Harrington, *American Population*, 136–38; *LP* 3:41.

10. Peter Kolchin, *American Slavery, 1619–1877* (New York, 1993), 63–92, for the uniqueness of the racial context in North America.

11. James Baldwin, *Notes of a Native Son* (New York, 1955), 34. The first historian to call attention to the linkage between ending slavery and the surge of racism was Jordan, *White over Black*. Duncan J. MacLeod, *Slavery, Race and the American Revolution* (Cambridge, U.K., 1974) and Nicholas Guyatt, *Bind Us Apart: How Enlightened Americans Invented Racial Segregation* (New York, 2016) developed the theme more fully, as did Edmund S. Morgan, *American Slavery, American Freedom: The Ordeal of Colonial Virginia* (New York, 1975). I was fortunate: Morgan was my mentor at Yale, and Jordan my teacher at William and Mary.

Chapter 2
ANGLES OF VISION

1. Charles Francis Adams, ed., *The Works of John Adams*, 10 vols. (Boston 1850–56), 1: introduction.

2. Quoted in Joseph J. Ellis, *Passionate Sage: The Character and Legacy of John Adams* (New York, 1993), 82.

3. Herbert Butterfield, *The Whig Interpretation of History* (Cambridge, U.K., 1931), 31–32.

4. David Brion Davis, *The Problem of Slavery in the Age of Revolution, 1770 1823* (New York, 1999), 255–56, 312–14.

5. Hannah Arendt, *On Revolution* (New York, 1963), 85–111, for the contrast between the American and French revolutions.

Chapter 3
THE CONTRADICTION

1. *PAR* 1:1–24.

2. Ibid., 25–40, for Bernard's *Principles*.

3. For obvious reasons, the scholarship on the emerging American resistance to British rule is massive. Two works are seminal: Edmund S. Morgan and Helen M. Morgan, *The Stamp Act Crisis: Prologue to Revolution* (Chapel Hill, N.C., 1953); and Bernard Bailyn, *The Ideological Origins of the American Revolution* (Cambridge, Mass., 1967). My effort at a sensible synthesis is provided in *The Cause: The American Revolution and Its Discontents, 1773–1783* (New York, 2021), 3–51.

4. The pamphlet literature, with a helpful overview by Gordon Wood, is available in *PAR* 1.

5. Gordon Wood, "The Problem of Sovereignty," *WMQ* 68 (Oct. 2011), 592–677.

6. The best synthesis of the British perspective is Andrew Jackson O'Shaughnessy, *The Men Who Lost America: British Leadership, the American Revolution, and the Fate of the Empire* (New Haven, 2013).

7. *PAR* 1:66–76, which contains the quotations in the previous two paragraphs.

8. GW to Bryan Fairfax, Aug. 24, 1774, *WW* 3:242.

9. *PAR* 2:496.

10. Patrick Henry to Robert Pleasants, Jan. 18, 1773, ms., Friends House, London, quoted in David Brion Davis, *The Problem of Slavery in the Age of Revolution* (New York, 1999), 196.

11. John Allen, *The Watchman's Alarm to Lord North* (Salem, Mass., 1774), 3–4.

12. Samuel Hopkins, *A Dialogue Concerning the Slavery of the Africans* (New York, 1776), 39.

13. Philip S. Foner, ed., *The Complete Writings of Thomas Paine*, 2 vols. (New York, 1945), 2–18.

14. John Chester Miller, *The Wolf by the Ears: Thomas Jefferson and Slavery* (New York, 1977), 4–5.

15. Eva Sheppard Wolf, *Race and Liberty in the New Nation* (Baton Rouge, 2006), 1–38, for the popular attitude toward emancipation in Virginia.

16. *Virginia Gazette*, Dec. 2, 1773, quoted in ibid., 17.

17. Edmund S. Morgan, "Slavery and Freedom: The American Paradox," *Journal of American History* (June 1972), 6.

18. The abovementioned book by Eva Sheppard Wolf provides the most persuasive case for this harsh but historically correct assessment of the Old Dominion, where I was born and raised.

19. See my treatment of this extended moment in *The Cause*, 30–33.

20. *Am Ar* 6:1618, 1623–29.

21. Ibid., 755, for Virginia's instructions to its delegates in Congress.

22. JA to John Winthrop, June 23, 1776, *AP* 4:332–33.

23. James Sullivan to JA, April 12, 1776, ibid., 208–12.

24. AA to JA, March 31, 1776, *AFC* 1:370.

25. AA to JA, March 31, 1776, ibid., 402.

26. Anonymous to JA, June 9, 1775, and Unknown to JA, Dec. 10, 1775; both in *AP* 3:18–19, 386.

27. Humanity to JA, Jan. 23, 1776, ibid., 411.

28. JA to Mercy Otis Warren, April 16, 1776, ibid., 4:124.

29. *LDC* 4:233–50 for the Dickinson Draft.

30. Ibid., 338–39.

31. *DA* 2:245–46; *JP* 1:320–23.

32. See my *Revolutionary Summer: The Birth of American Independence*

(New York, 2013), 212–13, for a synthesis of the argument over counting slaves.

33. *DA* 2:240; *JP* 1:323–27. Even though his title suggests otherwise, Jack N. Rakove's *The Beginnings of National Politics: An Interpretive History of the Continental Congress* (New York, 1979) most clearly demonstrates that the political unity required for winning the war was presumed by most delegates to be a provisional and temporary arrangement.

34. For the drafting of the Declaration, see Julian Boyd, *The Declaration of Independence: The Evolution of the Text* (Princeton, 1945); Pauline Maier, *American Scripture: Making the Declaration of Independence* (New York, 1997); and my effort in *American Sphinx: The Character of Thomas Jefferson* (New York, 1997), 36–53.

35. Merrill D. Peterson, ed., *The Portable Thomas Jefferson* (New York, 1975), 238–39, for the most accessible version of the Declaration in print. Jefferson's notes on the editorial changes made in his draft of the Declaration are in *JP* 1:314–15.

36. Peterson, ed., *Portable Jefferson*, 238.

37. Roy P. Basler, ed., *The Collected Works of Abraham Lincoln*, 9 vols. (New Brunswick, N.J., 1953–55), 3:376.

38. Speech, June 26, 1857, ibid., 2:408.

39. Garry Wills, *Inventing America: Jefferson's Declaration of Independence* (New York, 1978), 240–48, provides the fullest account of replacing "property" with "pursuit of happiness." Sean Wilentz, *No Property in Man: Slavery and Antislavery at the Nation's Founding* (Cambridge, Mass., 2018), emphasizes the historical significance of the verbal change in the subsequent debate over slavery.

Chapter 4
UNPAINTED PICTURES

1. Rick Atkinson is currently working on a trilogy that promises to provide a realistic account of what the late, great John Keegan called *The Face of Battle: A Study of Agincourt, Waterloo, and the Somme* (New York, 1976).

2. Paul Staiti, *Of Arms and Artists: The American Revolution Through Painters' Eyes* (New York, 2016), is the most comprehensive appraisal of the prominent American artists of the era.

3. AA to Elizabeth Smith Shaw, March 4, 1776, *AFC* 7:82.

4. Staiti, *Of Arms and Artists*, 178–83; Christian Di Spigna, *Founding Martyr: The Life and Death of Dr. Joseph Warren, the American Revolution's Lost Hero* (New York, 2018).

5. George Quintal, Jr., *Patriots of Color . . . at Battle Road and Bunker*

Hill (Lincoln, Maine, 2002). See also David Hackett Fischer, *African Founders* (New York, 2022), 79–80.

6. Council of War, Oct. 8, 1775, *PWR* 2:123–38; General Orders, Nov. 12, 1775, ibid., 353–55; GW to John Hancock, Dec. 31, 1775, ibid., 623.

7. Benjamin Quarles, *The Negro in the American Revolution* (Chapel Hill, N.C., 1961), is the pioneering scholarly work on that topic that has held up over the years with impressive accuracy.

8. *Am Ar* 5:1047–57, 6:461–62. Secondary accounts include Quarles, *Negro in the American Revolution*, 19–32; Gerald W. Mullin, *Flight and Rebellion: Slave Resistance in Eighteenth Century Virginia* (New York, 1972), 121–24; and more recently, Edward J. Larson, *American Inheritance: Liberty and Slavery in the Birth of a Nation, 1765–1795* (New York, 2023), 97–100, 124–25.

9. JM to William Bradford, June 19, 1775, *MP* 1:153. See Cassandra Pybus, *Epic Journeys of Freedom* (Boston, 2006), 8–9, for the historical context from the perspective of the runaway slaves.

10. *Am Ar* 5:816–20, for the debate in the House of Commons.

11. Ibid., 820–25. Although there was no official statement in the huge rulebook governing the organization of the British army prohibiting Blacks from serving alongside Whites in combat units, the tradition was sufficiently established that argument over the policy was unnecessary. On a few occasions during the war, black conscripts serving in support units as wagon masters or manservants to British officers were mobilized to confront battlefield emergencies, and usually performed admirably, but segregation remained the norm in the British army.

12. *Diary*, Sept. 24, 1775, *DA* 1:183.

13. See the multiple quotations from the Virginia press in Elizabeth A. Fenn, *Pox Americana: The Great Smallpox Epidemic of 1775–82* (New York, 2001), which estimates that a hundred thousand died of the disease; that number would probably be larger if escaped slaves were included in the mix.

14. *Virginia Gazette*, July 20, 1776. The gruesome scene is graphically depicted in Pybus, *Epic Journeys*, 17–19.

15. Richard Henry Lee to Catherine Macauley, Nov. 29, 1775, quoted in Larson, *American Inheritance*, 98; Woody Holton, *Forced Founders: Indians, Debtors, Slaves, and the Making of the Revolution in Virginia* (Chapel Hill, N.C., 1999), 159–60.

16. Eva Sheppard Wolf, *Race and Liberty in the New Nation: Emancipation in Virginia from the Revolution to Nat Turner's Rebellion* (Baton Rouge, 2006), for the prevailing presumptions of black inferiority within the white population of Virginia throughout the founding era.

17. Joseph Plumb Martin, *A Narrative of a Revolutionary Soldier* (New York,

2001), 144–45. Wayne Bodle, *The Valley Forge Winter: Civilians and Soldiers in War* (University Park, Pa., 2002), and Bob Drury and Tom Clavin, *Valley Forge* (New York, 2018), provide comprehensive overviews. My own effort at telling the story more briefly is in *The Cause: The American Revolution and Its Discontents, 1773–1783* (New York, 2021), 152–90.

18. GW to HL, Dec. 23, 1777, *PWRS* 12:683.

19. Two of the most important books on the government under the Articles of Confederation announce in their titles the exact opposite of what the Articles created: Jack N. Rakove, *The Beginnings of National Politics: An Interpretive History of the Continental Congress* (New York, 1979), and Merrill Jensen, *The New Nation: A History of the United States During the Confederation, 1781–1789* (New York, 1950).

20. See David C. Hendrickson, *Peace Pact: The Lost World of the American Founding* (Lawrence, Kans., 2003).

21. GW to Benjamin Harrison, March 4, 1783, *WW* 26:184–85.

22. For a more robust account of the state-based mentality, see my effort in *The Quartet: Orchestrating the Second American Revolution, 1783–1789* (New York, 2015), 5–28.

23. Arthur Zilversmit, *The First Emancipation: The Abolition of Slavery in the North* (Chicago, 1967), is old but still reliable. More recent, and more focused on the role of African Americans, are Paul J. Polgar, *Standard-Bearers of Equality: America's First Abolition Movement* (Chapel Hill, N.C., 2019), and Kate Masur, *Until Justice Be Done: America's First Civil Rights Movement, from the Revolution to Reconstruction* (New York, 2021).

24. Edmund Randolph, *History of Virginia* (Charlottesville, Va., 1970), 252–53.

25. *Pennsylvania Packet,* Feb. 17, 1780, for the quotation. See also Edmund Raymond Turner, "The Abolition of Slavery in Pennsylvania," *Pennsylvania Journal of History and Biography* 36, no. 2 (1912), 137.

26. Gary B. Nash and Jean R. Soderlund, *Freedom by Degrees: Emancipation in Philadelphia and Its Aftermath* (New York, 1991), is the best scholarly synthesis.

27. *WW* 13:43, ed. note, for Germain's orders to Clinton. For a full account of British deliberations, see my effort in *The Cause,* 196–98.

28. GW to President of Congress, March 15, 1779, *WW* 14:241–45.

29. John Laurens to HL, Feb. 2, 1778, *LDC* 12:390–93; AH to JJ, March 14, 1779, *HP* 2:18.

30. John Laurens to GW, May 19, 1782, *WW* 16:221.

31. *WAR,* 152–59, provides the terms of Rutledge's surrender offer and excellent maps of the Charleston siege. See also John S. Pancake, *The Destruc-*

tive War: The British Campaign in the Carolinas, 1780–1782 (Tuscaloosa, Ala., 1985), 56–72.

32. Clinton's proclamation was published in *The Royal Gazette* (1779). It promised refuge for all runaways and implied freedom for all slaves who performed well as laborers in the British army. It failed to mention that runaways owned by loyalists would be returned.

33. Whipple quoted in *Magazine of American History* (1889), 63–64.

34. Cornwallis to Henry Clinton, Dec. 4, 1781, in *The Cornwallis Papers: The Campaign of 1780 and 1781 in the Southern Theatre of the American Revolutionary War,* 6 vols., ed. Ian Saberton (Ashfield, Ireland, 2010), 3:27028. For the chaotic character of the war in the southern theater, see Pancake, *Destructive War,* and W. Robert Higgins, ed., *The Revolutionary War in the South: Power, Conflict, and Leadership* (Durham, N.C., 1979).

35. The authoritative source for this stage of the Carolina campaign, and for Cornwallis's posture toward runaways, is Sylvia R. Frey, *Water from the Rock: Black Resistance in a Revolutionary Age* (Princeton, 1991), 109–36.

36. Johann Ewald, *Diary of the American War: A Hessian Journal,* trans. and ed. Joseph P. Tustin (New Haven, 1979), 305.

37. Charles Cornwallis to Henry Clinton, April 12, 1781, in Saberton, ed., *Cornwallis Papers,* 6:317–18.

38. For Clinton's official report on Arnold's Virginia campaign, see William B. Willcox, *Portrait of a General: Sir Henry Clinton and the War of Independence* (New York, 1964), 370–71.

39. GW to TJ, June 8, 1781, *WW* 22:178–79.

40. Quoted in Larson, *American Inheritance,* 145, which provides an account of the debate in the Virginia legislature regarding the recruitment of enslaved troops that most historians, including this one, have missed.

41. James Jones to JM, Jan. 17, 1781, *MP* 2:293; TJ to William Gordon, July 16, 1788, *JP* 13:364. Most recently, Alan Taylor has estimated that approximately four thousand slaves fled to Cornwallis in 1781. See Taylor's *American Revolution: A Continental History, 1750–1804* (New York, 2016), 240–41.

42. GW to Robert Howe, Sept. 24, 1781, *WW* 23:132. For the Battle of the Chesapeake, see Nathaniel Philbrick, *In the Hurricane's Eye: The Genius of George Washington and the Victory at Yorktown* (New York, 2018), 204–39.

43. GW to President of Congress, Oct. 16, 1781, *WW* 23:227–29, provides the official report on the attack led by Hamilton and Laurens.

44. Martin, *Narrative of a Revolutionary Soldier,* 198–99.

45. In his pioneering work *Negroes in the American Revolution,* Benjamin Quarles estimated the number of runaways at "tens of thousands." My educated guess, based on the unrecorded losses, amplified the number

to "many tens," which concurs with Sylvia Frey's assessment in *Water from the Rock*. Cassandra Pybus in *Epic Journeys* disagrees, putting the number much lower, at twenty thousand. Her research is impeccable, but Pybus is devoted to telling the stories of the runaways whose journeys ended in the promised land. I prefer to provide equal treatment to those who never made it.

46. Articles of Capitulation quoted in Philbrick, *In the Hurricane's Eye*, 235. The most detailed description of the surrender is Thomas J. Fleming, *The Perils of Peace: America's Struggle for Survival After Yorktown* (New York, 2007), 8–12. For the Hessian officer's remark, see Ludwig von Closen, *The Revolutionary Journal of Baron Ludwig von Closen, 1780–83* (Chapel Hill, N.C., 1958), 138–42.

47. Cornwallis quoted in Stanley Weintraub, *Iron Tears: America's Battle for Freedom, Britain's Quagmire* (New York, 2005), 311; Ian R. Christie, *The End of North's Ministry, 1780–1782* (London, 1958), 340–42.

48. Graves quoted in Piers Mackesy, *The War for America, 1775–1783* (Cambridge, Mass., 1964), 252.

49. Gregory D. Massey, *John Laurens and the American Revolution* (Columbia, S.C., 2000), 225–28.

50. Richard B. Morris, *The Peacemakers: The Great Powers and American Independence* (New York, 1965), 382.

51. For Carleton's correspondence with Leslie on "the Negro question," see Pybus, *Epic Journeys,* 58–59. Conveniently unmentioned by both Carleton and Leslie was the fact that the promise of emancipation was contingent on Great Britain's winning the war.

52. GW to Daniel Parker, April 28, 1783, *WW* 26:364.

53. Conference between GW and Sir Gary Carleton, May 6, 1783, ibid., 402–3; Commissioners of Embarkation to GW, Jan. 18, 1784, *PWCS* 1:50–56; GW to Benjamin Harrison, April 30, 1783, *WW* 26:370.

54. Dorothy Twohig, "'That Species of Property': Washington's Role in the Controversy Over Slavery," in Don Higgenbotham, ed., *George Washington Reconsidered* (Charlottesville, Va., 2001), 114–38, first called attention to the role that his legacy played in Washington's thought process regarding slavery.

55. My account of the evacuation is a synthesis based on the following studies: Quarles, *Negro in the American Revoluion*, 158–81; Frey, *Water from the Rock*, 174–93; Pybus, *Epic Journeys,* 57–72; and Larson, *American Inheritance*, 149–56.

56. My estimates track the numbers in Quarles, *Negro in the American Revolution*, and Frey, *Water from the Rock*. They are higher than the numbers provided in Pybus, *Epic Journeys*.

57. GW, Address to the Congress on Resigning His Commission, Dec. 23, 1783, *WW* 26:284–86.
58. TJ to Joseph Jones, April 16, 1784, *JP* 7:106–7.
59. Elkanah Watson, *Men and Times of the Revolution* (New York, 1856), 227.
60. AH to JJ, July 25, 1783, *HP* 3:416–17.
61. Joseph Clay to James Jackson, Feb. 16, 1784, quoted in Frey, *Water from the Rock,* 202.

Chapter 5
THE GHOST AT THE BANQUET

1. Samuel Flagg Bemis, *The Diplomacy of the American Revolution* (Bloomington, Ind., 1957), 212–13; Richard B. Morris, *The Peacemakers: The Great Powers and American Independence* (New York, 1965), 309–10.
2. *WW* 26:492–96.
3. See my *His Excellency: George Washington* (New York, 2004), 151–57, for a fuller account of Washington's western vision. See also Don Higgenbotham, ed., *George Washington Reconsidered* (Charlottesville, Va., 2001), 198–211.
4. Deed of the Virginia Cession, March 1, 1784, *JP* 6:578.
5. Ibid., 580–616; *JCC* 26:118–20, 255–60.
6. The following argument borrows heavily from research that I did for *The Quartet: Orchestrating the Second American Revolution, 1783–1789* (New York, 2015).
7. JJ to Richard Henry Lee, Jan. 23, 1785, *JP* 4; JJ to JA, Nov. 1, 1786, ibid., 6.
8. Resolution Calling for a Convention, July 20, 1782, *HP* 3:110–13. For the fate of Hamilton's resolution, see JCC 23:476, 24:285, 25:523.
9. JM to TJ, Aug. 12, 1786, *MP* 9:46; JM to James Monroe, March 14, 1786, *MP* 8:497–98.
10. Address at the Annapolis Convention, Sept. 14, 1786, *HP* 3:687–89.
11. JM to GW, Nov. 8, 1786, *MP* 9:166–67.
12. GW to JJ, Aug. 15, 1786, *PWCS* 4:213.
13. GW to Lafayette, May 10, 1786, ibid., 42; GW to Henry Knox, Feb. 25, 1787, *PWCS* 5:52–53.
14. GW to James Warren, Oct. 7, 1785, *PWCS* 3:299; GW to JM, Nov. 10, 1785, ibid., 420.
15. GW to AH, March 3, 1783, *PWCS* 1:276–77.
16. GW to JM, March 20, 1787, *PWFC* 5:94–95, 114–17.
17. JM to Edmund Randolph, April 8, 1787, *MP* 9:368; JM to GW, April 16, 1787, ibid., 383.

18. "Notes on Ancient and Modern Confederacies," April–June, 1786, ibid., 3–24.
19. "Vices of the Political System of the United States," ibid., 345–58.
20. "James Madison at the Federal Convention," ed. note, *MP* 10:3–10.
21. JM to TJ, June 6, 1787, ibid., 29–30.
22. "Virginia Plan," May 29, 1787, ibid., 15–17.
23. My version of the historical context at the convention draws upon five secondary accounts by distinguished historians: Max Farrand, *The Framing of the Constitution of the United States* (New Haven, 1913), which is old but venerable; Catherine Drinker Bowen, *Miracle at Philadelphia: The Story of the Constitutional Convention, May to September 1787* (Boston, 1966), which lacks notes but provides the most narrative verve; Jack N. Rakove, *Original Meanings: Politics and Ideas in the Making of the Constitution* (New York, 1996), which is less a narrative than a compelling, topically organized analysis; Carol Berkin, *A Brilliant Solution: Inventing the American Constitution* (New York, 2003), the most succinct account, also written with a nice edge; and, finally, Richard Beeman, *Plain, Honest Men: The Making of the American Constitution* (New York, 2009), a truly superb scholarly synthesis, comprehensive and, in my judgment, the most persuasive on the slavery issue.
24. Gaillard Hunt and James Brown Scott, eds., *The Debates in the Federal Convention of 1787 . . . Reported by James Madison* (New York, 1920), 18–21. Hereafter cited as *Debates*.
25. Ibid., 21–23.
26. Mary Sarah Bilder, *Madison's Hand: Revising the Constitutional Convention* (Cambridge, Mass., 2015).
27. Precisely because David Waldstreicher's *Slavery's Constitution: From Revolution to Ratification* (New York, 2009) embraces the uncompromising moralistic perspective of the Quaker abolitionists in the nineteenth century, who were fully prepared to let the slave states "go in peace," his account of the convention is most alert to the indirect ways in which the Constitution endorsed a proslavery agenda.
28. Madison quoted in Max Farrand, ed., *The Records of the Federal Convention of 1787*, 4 vols. (New Haven, 1937), 1:486–87. Two books by distinguished nineteenth-century historians, *No Property in Man: Slavery and Antislavery at the Nation's Founding* (Cambridge, Mass., 2018) by Sean Wilentz, and *The Crooked Path to Abolition: Abraham Lincoln and the Antislavery Constitution* (New York, 2021) by James Oakes, keenly present an antislavery interpretation of the Constitution as Abraham Lincoln viewed it. Lincoln, of course, had some powerful political reasons to downplay the proslavery side, which, as I see it, was shaped by

powerful political reasons to defer the slavery question until the infant American republic had outgrown its infancy.

29. GW to AH, July 10, 1787, *PWCS* 5:257.

30. Beeman, *Plain, Honest Men*, 146–62, provides the best account of this extended moment.

31. Ibid., 188–97.

32. JM to TJ, Sept. 6, 1787, *MP* 10:163–66.

33. David C. Hendrickson, *Peace Pact: The Lost World of the American Founding* (Lawrence, Kans., 2003), 40–47, for the prevailing dread of monarchy.

34. *Debates*, 18–21; *HP* 4:181 for Hamilton's speech. See also Ron Chernow, *Alexander Hamilton* (New York, 2004), 231.

35. Dickinson quoted in James H. Hudson, ed., *A Supplement to Max Farrand's Records of the Federal Convention of 1797* (New Haven, 1987), 158.

36. Beeman, *Plain, Honest Men*, 107–32.

37. Farrand, ed., *Records*, 152–54, 370.

38. Staughton Lynd, "The Compromise of 1787," *Political Science Quarterly* 81 (1966), 225–50; Lawrence Goldstone, *Dark Bargain: Slavery, Profits, and the Struggle for the Constitution* (New York, 2005); Beeman, *Plain, Honest Men*, 185–87.

39. Farrand, ed., *Records*, 2:221–23.

40. Ibid., 1:244, 152–54, 370.

41. Ibid., 2:364–65.

42. John P. Kaminski, ed., *A Necessary Evil?: Slavery and the Debate over the Constitution* (Madison, Wisc., 1995), 62–64.

43. Ibid., 65.

44. Franklin's speech is reprinted in Edmund S. Morgan, ed., *Not Your Usual Founding Father: Selected Readings from Benjamin Franklin* (New Haven, 2006), 286–87.

45. Richard Brookhiser, *Gentleman Revolutionary: Gouverneur Morris, the Rake Who Wrote the Constitution* (New York, 2003), 92.

Chapter 6
THE EPILOGUE

1. The essential primary source is *DHRC*, the documentary history of the debate in all the states. The authoritative secondary account is Pauline Maier, *Ratification: The People Debate the Constitution, 1787–1788* (New York, 2010). For the debate over slavery, John Kaminski, ed., *A Necessary Evil?: Slavery and the Debate over the Constitution* (Madison, Wisc.,

1994), is an excellent guide to the different conventions and the press coverage in all the states.

2. The chart originally appeared in my earlier effort at explaining the ratification process, *The Quartet: Orchestrating the American Revolution* (New York, 2015), 173.

3. Marshall quoted in Jean Edward Smith, *John Marshall: Definer of a Nation* (New York, 1996), 118.

4. JM to Ambrose Madison, Sept. 30, 1787, *MP* 10:179–80.

5. JM to TJ, Oct. 24, 1787, ibid., 208.

6. Maier, *Ratification,* 155–211. The proposed amendments are best discussed in Saul Cornell, *The Other Founders: Anti-Federalism and the Dissenting Tradition in America, 1788–1828* (Chapel Hill, N.C., 1999), 30–31.

7. The physical description of Madison is in Drew R. McCoy, *The Last of the Founders: James Madison and the Republican Legacy* (Cambridge, U.K., 1989). Jefferson's comment on Patrick Henry is in TJ to JM, Dec. 8, 1784, *RL* 1:353–54.

8. *DHRC* 9:952–61, 995–96, 1028–31.

9. Kaminski, ed., *Necessary Evil,* 187.

10. Ibid., 187–88.

11. Ibid., 95–99.

12. Ibid., 67–70.

13. Ibid., 136–37.

14. Ibid., 169.

15. Ibid., 170.

16. Ibid., 171.

17. Linda Grant DePauw et al., eds., *Documentary History of the First Federal Congress of the United States,* 15 vols. (Baltimore, 1972), 12:277–87.

18. Ibid., 287–88.

19. Ibid., 289–90.

20. Ibid., 291.

21. DePauw et al., eds., *First Congress,* 3:294. The text of Franklin's petition is more readily available in Kaminski, ed., *Necessary Evil,* 147–48.

22. DePauw et al., eds., *First Congress,* 12:307–8.

23. Ibid., 308–10.

24. Ibid., 297–98, 310–11.

25. Ibid., 295–96, 307. There are several versions of the debate recorded in *First Congress,* based on newspaper accounts at the time. In places, the chronology is uneven.

26. Ibid., 12:649–62.

27. Ibid., 719–21.

28. Ibid., 725–35.

29. The scholarship on Franklin defies succinct summary. When I reached

thirteen books and seven essays, I decided to stop making a list, in part because I realized the list was only a start, in part because I felt like I was committing the sin of conspicuous erudition, and heard Franklin laughing at me.

30. Albert H. Smyth, ed., *The Writings of Benjamin Franklin,* 10 vols. (New York, 1907), 10:87–91.

31. DePauw et al., eds., *First Congress,* 12:809–12, 825–91.

32. JM to Edmund Randolph, March 21, 1790, *MP,* 13:109–10.

33. JM to Benjamin Rush, March 20, 1790, ibid., 109. The shrewdest assessment of Madison's inherently equivocal language and thought process about slavery is McCoy, *Last of the Founders,* 217–20.

34. DePauw et al., eds., *First Congress,* 3:338–41.

35. Ibid., 342.

36. For the petition of 1792 and Smith's reaction, see *Annals of Congress,* 2nd Congress, 2nd Session, 728–31. For the Webster comment, see Daniel Webster to John Bolton, May 17, 1833, in *The Papers of Daniel Webster,* ed. Charles M. Wiltse, 7 vols. (Hanover, N.H., 1974–86), 3:252–53. For Lincoln's interpretation of his limited authority to address the slavery issue in the existent southern states, see my summary of the scholarly literature in *American Dialogue: The Founders and Us* (New York, 2018), 5–6. The most recent review of Lincoln's view of the founding legacy on slavery is James Oakes, *The Crooked Path to Abolition: Abraham Lincoln and the Antislavery Constitution* (New York, 2021).

37. DePauw et al., eds., *First Congress,* 3:375.

38. John Craig Hammond, *Slavery, Freedom, and Expansion in the Early American West* (Charlottesville, Va., 2007), provides a much more detailed story of the Kentucky precedent.

Chapter 7
THE TREATY

1. Bernard W. Sheehan, "Indian-White Relations in Early America: A Review Essay," *WMQ* 26 (April 1969), 267–86. See also Frederick E. Hoxie, Ronald Hoffman, and Peter J. Albert, eds., *Native Americans and the Early Republic* (Charlottesville, Va., 1999).

2. Daniel K. Richter, *Facing East from Indian Country: A Native History of Early America* (Cambridge, Mass., 2001). For the Indian quotation, see ed. note, *PWPS* 10:190–94.

3. Henry Knox to GW, June 15, 1789, *PWPS* 2:489–95.

4. Henry Knox to GW, Jan. 4, 1790, ibid., 4:529–36.

5. The two standard works are Francis P. Prucha, *American Indian Policy in the Formative Years: The Indian Trade and Intercourse Acts, 1790–*

1834 (Cambridge, Mass., 1962), and Reginald Horsman, *Expansion and American Indian Policy, 1783–1812* (East Lansing, Mich., 1967).

6. For the treaties, see *AIUS* 4:2267–77.

7. Horsman, *Expansion and American Indian Policy,* 22.

8. Philip Schuyler to President of Congress, July 29, 1783, *JCC* 3:601–7. Washington endorsed the Schuyler strategy in GW to James Duane, Sept. 7, 1783, *WW* 27:133–40.

9. *AIUS* 2:2140–43. See also Prucha, *American Indian Policy,* 36–39.

10. *AIUS* 2:2144–50.

11. Arthur St. Clair to GW, May 2, 1789, *PWPS* 2:198–200.

12. Henry Knox to GW, July 7, 1789, ibid., 3:138–40.

13. Ibid., 141.

14. Arthur St. Clair to GW, May 2, 1789, ibid., 2:198–200.

15. Henry Knox to GW, July 28, 1789, ibid., 3:337–38.

16. Henry Knox to GW, June 15, 1789, ibid., 2:494.

17. *DHFC* 2:31–36.

18. Ibid., 9:128–32.

19. John W. Caughey, *McGillivray of the Creeks* (Norman, Okla., 1938), 3–57, an introductory essay followed by McGillivray's correspondence.

20. See letter of July 10, 1785, in ibid., 90–91.

21. Ibid., 3–57.

22. David Humphreys to GW, Sept. 26, 1789, *PWPS* 4:86–89; McGillivray letter of Oct. 8, 1789, in Caughey, *McGillivray,* 251–54.

23. *PWPS* 4:86–89, note 3.

24. Letter of Oct. 12, 1780, in Caughey, *McGillivray,* 255.

25. Henry Knox to GW, Oct. 27, 1789, *PWPS* 4:248.

26. GW's Memoranda on Indian Affairs, Dec. 1789, ibid., 4:468–94.

27. Henry Knox to GW, Feb. 15, 1790, ibid., 5:140–47.

28. For the most recent synthesis of the Yazoo claims, see Richter, *Facing East from Indian Country,* 226–28.

29. See letter of May 8, 1790, in Caughey, *McGillivray,* 259–62.

30. Letter of May 20, 1790, in ibid., 263.

31. Letter of March 6, 1790, in ibid., 256–58.

32. Letter of May 8, 1790, in ibid., 261.

33. *New York Daily Gazette,* July 3, 17, 19, 21, and 22, 1790.

34. For McGillivray's statements of confidence in his Creek warriors and the inherent fragility of the American republic, see Caughey, *McGillivray,* 130–32, 172–74, 182.

35. See *PWPS* 6:104, note 2, for the episode with the Trumbull painting.

36. For the most penetrating study of the subject, see Anthony F. C. Wallace, *Jefferson and the Indians: The Tragic Fate of the First Americans* (Cambridge, Mass., 1999).

37. Opinion of Certain Georgia Land Grants, May 3, 1790, *JP* 17:288–91.
38. Merrill D. Peterson, ed., *The Portable Thomas Jefferson* (New York, 1975), 23–232, provides the most accessible edition of *Notes*. The discussion of Indians is found in ibid., 93–103, 133–50.
39. Ibid., 96–99.
40. Caughey, *McGillivray*, 46. See also the letter of Feb. 26, 1791, in ibid., 288–89, in which McGillivray reiterated his focus on the Yazoo threat.
41. GW to United States Senate, Aug. 7, 1790, *PWPS* 6:213–14; Jackson's remarks in Caughey, *McGillivray*, 45.
42. *AIUS* 4:2206–88.
43. Ibid., 2290.
44. Ibid., 2288.
45. GW to United States Senate, Aug. 4, 1790, *PWPS* 6:188–96.
46. *National Advertiser and Gazette of the United States*, Aug. 14 1790. See also *PWPS* 6:253–54; Caughey, *McGillivray*, 278–79.
47. GW to Tobias Lear, April 3, 1791, and GW to AH, April 4, 1791, *PWPS* 8:49, 57–58. For the "Chinese wall" reference, see GW to Secretary of State, July 1, 1796, *WW* 35:11.
48. For troop estimates necessary to control the frontier, see *PWPS* 6:362–65, 668–70; *PWPS* 8:200–225; *PWPS* 9:37–41, 158–68.

Chapter 8
REGRETS AT MOUNT VERNON

1. *PWRT* 4:512–27.
2. Mary V. Thompson, *"The Only Unavoidable Subject of Regret": George Washington, Slavery, and the Enslaved Community at Mount Vernon* (Charlottesville, Va., 2019), 314–19.
3. Robert Pleasants to GW, Dec. 11, 1785, *PWCS* 3:449–19.
4. GW to Francis Hopkinson, May 16, 1785, *PWCS* 2:561–62; ed. note, ibid., 508–9. For the Houdon visit, see TJ to GW, Dec. 10, 1784, ibid., 176–78. My earlier effort at covering this moment is in *His Excellency: George Washington* (New York, 2004), 154.
5. GW to Lafayette, Dec. 8, 1784, *PWCS* 2:175–76, on the aging theme; see also the correspondence in ibid., 386–90, *PWCS* 3:50, and *PWCS* 4:126.
6. Rosemarie Zagarri, ed., *David Humphreys' "Life of General Washington" with Washington's "Remarks"* (Athens, Ga., 1991), 78. See also Henry Wiencek, *An Imperfect God: George Washington, His Slaves, and the Creation of America* (New York, 2003), 272. Though I disagree with Wiencek on this issue, let me add that his book on Washington and slavery set a new scholarly standard for that controversial topic.
7. GW to Alexander Spotswood, Nov. 23 1784, *WW* 34:47–48.

8. GW to Tobias Lear, May 6, 1794, ibid., 33:358.
9. Thompson, *Only Unavoidable Subject*, 285–89, and Wiencek, *Imperfect God*, 311–34, both provide detailed coverage of the Ona Judge episode.
10. GW to Joseph Whipple, Nov. 18, 1796, *WW* 35:297.
11. Schedule of Property, June 1799, *PWRT* 4:477–511. The first scholars to emphasize the distributive implications of the will were Robert and Lee Dalzell, *George Washington's Mount Vernon: At Home in Revolutionary America* (New York, 1998), 220–22.
12. Philip J. Schwarz, ed., *Slavery at the Home of George Washington* (Mount Vernon, 2001), 159–79, for the role of the Mount Vernon Ladies' Association.

Chapter 9
MEMORIES AT MONTICELLO

1. Auguste Levasseur, *Lafayette in America, 1824–1826*, 2 vols. (Philadelphia, 1829), 1:217–19.
2. Gilbert Chinard, ed., *The Letters of Lafayette and Thomas Jefferson* (Baltimore, 1929), 359.
3. *Columbian Centinel*, Oct. 20, 1824, reprinted in Nicholas Guyatt, *Bind Us Apart* (New York, 2016), 276.
4. Lafayette to GW, July 14, 1785, *PWCS* 3:121; GW to Lafayette, May 10, 1786, ibid., 4:43–4, for Washngton's endorsement of Lafayette's experiment in Cayenne.
5. The quotations from *Notes* are available in Merrill D. Peterson, ed., *The Portable Thomas Jefferson* (New York, 1975), 186–93, 214–15.
6. See my *American Dialogue: The Founding Fathers and Us* (New York, 2018), 35–44, for a more expansive account of Jefferson's reaffirmation of black inferiority and "expatriation" during his retirement years.
7. TJ to Jared Sparks, Feb. 4, 1784, *JP* 10:289–93.
8. Merrill D. Peterson, ed., *Visitors to Monticello* (Charlottesville, Va., 1957), 30, for the quotation. See also Lucia C. Stanton, "'Those Who Labor for My Happiness': Thomas Jefferson and His Slaves," in *Jeffersonian Legacies*, ed. Peter S. Onuf (Charlottesville, Va., 1993), 151–59.
9. Levasseur, *Lafayette in America*, 1:211–12. See also Susan Dunn, *Dominion of Memories: Jefferson, Madison, and the Decline of Virginia* (New York, 2007), 1–12.
10. Ellen Randolph Coolidge to TJ, Aug. 1 1825, in *The Family Letters of Thomas Jefferson*, ed. Edwin Morris Betts and James Adam Bear, Jr. (Charlottesville, 1995), 454–57.
11. TJ to Ellen Coolidge, Aug. 27, 1825, in ibid., 457–58.

12. TJ to James Monroe, March 8, 1826, *JP* 10:383.
13. TJ to Roger C. Weightman, June 24, 1826, ibid., 390–92.
14. Eva Sheppard Wolf, *Race and Liberty in the New Nation: Emancipation in Virginia from the Revolution to Nat Turner's Rebellion* (Baton Rouge, 2006), 235–47.
15. Thomas Dew, *Review of the Debates in the Virginia Legislature* (Williamsburg, Va., 1832).
16. Dunn, *Dominion of Memories*, 12–26.

Index

A NOTE ABOUT THE AUTHOR

JOSEPH J. ELLIS is the author of thirteen works of American history, including *Founding Brothers: The Revolutionary Generation,* which was awarded the Pulitzer Prize, and *American Sphinx: The Character of Thomas Jefferson,* which won the National Book Award. He lives on Hawk Mountain, in Plymouth County, with his wife and two labradoodles.

A NOTE ON THE TYPE

This book was set in a modern adaptation of a type designed by the first William Caslon (1692–1766). The Caslon face, an artistic, easily read type, has enjoyed more than two centuries of popularity in the English-speaking world. This version, with its even balance and honest letterforms, was designed by Carol Twombly for the Adobe Corporation and released in 1990.

Composed by North Market Street Graphics,
Lancaster, Pennsylvania

Designed by Cassandra J. Pappas